10649957

CAN YOU
SEE MY
SCARS?

www.mascotbooks.com

Can You See My Scars?

Scripture quotations are from the ESV® Bible (The Holy Bible, English Standard Version®), copyright © 2001 by Crossway Bibles, a publishing ministry of Good News Publishers. Used by permission. All rights reserved.

This book is a memoir. The author has tried to recreate events, locales, and conversations from his memories of them. Additionally, for the sake of the story, some events have been compressed. In order to maintain their anonymity, in some instances the author has changed the names of individuals and places. The author may have changed some identifying characteristics and details such as physical properties, occupations, and places of residence. The author does not assume and hereby disclaims any liability to any party for any loss, damage, or disruption caused by errors or omissions, whether such errors or omissions result from negligence, accident, or any other cause.

Cover design by Nathaniel Navratil.
Author photograph by Tim Coburn Photography.

For more information, please contact:
Mascot Books
620 Herndon Parkway #320
Herndon, VA 20170
info@mascotbooks.com

Library of Congress Control Number: 2020904400

CPSIA Code: PRFRE0520A
ISBN-13: 978-1-64543-367-5

Printed in Canada

Dedicated to my mother, father, brother,
and sister, who were there for me every step of the way.

I love you all more than words could ever express.

And to my darling Megan, for her support, patience, and love.

CAN YOU SEE MY
SCARS?

My Unexpected Journey with Trauma, Burns, and Recovery

SAMUEL MOORE-SOBEL

PROLOGUE

No one knows what's going to happen next.
—L. Frank Baum, *The Patchwork Girl of Oz*

This is not a story I ever wanted to write.

I expected that my late teens and early twenties would contain certain milestones: graduating from college, starting a career, buying a home, and maybe even finding someone to love. I did not anticipate that those years would also hold something vastly different—an accident.

My accident, and the recovery process that followed, are detailed in the pages of this book. Some things have been left out, due to space constraints, but for the most part, these chapters tell the story of the day that changed my life forever and, subsequently, the ways in which I have healed. It is not my intention to glorify the choices I made—in fact, I try to highlight the many instances in which I made the wrong decision, or at least could have handled circumstances differently. The purpose of this book is simply to share my experience with you. My hope is that you find something useful for your own journey.

I've learned that much of suffering is universal and adversity is a great equalizer. They have ways of reaching us all whether we like it or not. The question is not so much if trials will come, but how we handle them when they arrive.

My story begins with a cardboard box. How could a simple cardboard box change my life forever, you ask? Just like anything else, I suppose. In an instant and all at once.

THAT FATEFUL DAY

Life can only be understood backwards;
but it must be lived forwards.
—Soren Kierkegaard

Tuesday, September 1, 2009, began like any other day. The morning was clear and sunny, warm even at an early hour. I had one more week until school was scheduled to begin, and I was intent on working my last odd job for the season. Sophomore year was just around the corner, and I felt optimistic at the thought of no longer being on the lowest rung of the high school totem pole.

The summer had been a productive one. I spent the months before September 1 working as a camp counselor. Once camp ended, I worked a variety of odd jobs for people in my community until school resumed. I welcomed the opportunity to earn some spending money before homework and extracurricular school activities occupied my time.

On that September day, I embarked on a job that I learned about from a man who lived a few blocks from my house. I assumed he had contacted me because he had either seen my name in the community newsletter's "Odd Job Squad," where I was just one of the forty-three young people listed as ready for work around the neighborhood; or, he had seen the flyers I had recently passed out to every house on his street advertising my availability to complete various odd jobs on behalf of residents.

The man asked me to complete a task that sounded simple enough: pack up a garage filled with items and transport them to a local storage unit.

A few days earlier, the same man had asked me to stop by his home to assess how much time I thought it would take to complete the project.

When I arrived to check out the project on Friday, August 28, I noticed the imposing figure of the man. He was tall, with streaked gray and white hair. After I shook his hand, he launched into conversation. He told me about his previous military service and his political views. He asked me what my political affiliation was and that of my family. He continued talking as he directed me toward the garage.

Upon further inspection, the job appeared much bigger than advertised, far more than a middle-aged man could complete even with the help of a teenager. The garage was filled to the brim with miscellaneous items: Amway purchases, containers filled with tax returns, assorted pieces of furniture. The man ruffled through various items, telling me about each one.

We discussed a project schedule starting Monday, August 31. He said he would rent a U-Haul truck, which would allow us to transport the large items housed within his garage. I agreed to begin the job at 9 a.m., and he estimated that we would be done by approximately 1 p.m. We discussed the possibility of inviting a third pair of hands to join us. After I left, I enlisted my friend Blake for help.

Two days later, on Sunday, August 30, the man called to cancel for August 31. He mentioned rain being in the forecast as his reason for rescheduling before asking if I would be available to assist on September 1. I readily agreed to the change and informed Blake of the adjustment in schedule.

On the appointed day, the streak of sunlight enveloping the morning sky led me to believe that the job would go quickly, allowing me to be home after lunch in order to prepare to host a friend for dinner that evening.

Upon our arrival, the man introduced Blake and me to his wife. Soon after, we got to work emptying his garage of items as instructed. Shortly thereafter, he informed us of a change in plans. Instead of moving the contents of the garage to the storage unit, we were now supposed to empty the contents of the storage unit and bring all of his belongings back to the house. He cited a desire to save money as his reason for clearing out the storage unit. Then he mentioned something about taking certain items to a friend's house to store in her shed. I was confused. Had I gotten the details wrong in the original plan?

We arrived at the storage unit by way of the rented U-Haul and began to empty the contents of the unit into the back of the truck. The unit was filled with extraneous items, much like the garage back at the man's house. As we lugged pieces of furniture and other assorted items, Blake and I initiated conversation with the man. He offered a few stories about his military service and described his current government job.

As the day wore on, the man continued making disparaging comments about President Obama. His outlook on the future of America was grim, based on the current political climate. He also shared negative views about being a landlord, detailing difficult encounters with a tenant in a townhome he and his wife had once owned and rented out.

After our work was complete, the man received his refund of a previous payment from the storage facility. "Now we have enough money to pay you guys," he said, adding something about how God provides.

Samuel Moore-Sobel

BORN TO ASK

Call to me and I will answer you, and will tell you
great and hidden things that you have not known.
—Jeremiah 33:3

My early life was, in some ways, a blur. My parents say that I was a precocious child who never stopped moving, which made it challenging for them to capture and maintain my attention. They employed a strategy that involved asking me as many questions as possible to distract me from my tendency to wander. I often responded to their questions with more questions of my own, posing many of them to my father.

As I got older, my questions for my father only increased. "How do you feel about that, Dad?" I would repeatedly ask him. Usually I asked silly things, and sometimes would ask the same question over and over. To this day, it drives my father crazy. He struggled to understand why I asked him so many questions—until we discovered a videotape of myself at eighteen months old.

In it, I mill about, unable to sit still even for a moment. My parents were days away from a trip to Europe and were attempting to prepare me for their two-week absence. They recorded a video of themselves reading my favorite books to calm me down during their time abroad. I am not sure it worked. The video shows baby Samuel unwilling to sit still. My stuffed animals are all assembled, with my favorite—the large, yellow Big Bird—placed prominently in the front. The stuffed animals, however, did not interest me as much as running around did.

My restlessness took root in childhood. I didn't believe in boredom. I kept myself entertained with constant movement—and *The Washington Post*. One of my earliest memories is of being greeted in the morning by a front-page picture of a man with gray hair sitting in a chair next to a woman who appeared to have tears in her eyes. I pondered the reason behind her tears. The caption underneath the photo identified the man as Regis Philbin and the woman as Kathy Lee Gifford. The headline revealed that Gifford was leaving the show. *Why was she leaving*? I wondered. *If it made her sad, shouldn't she just stay*?

I read the article, which answered some of my most burning questions, but left others completely untouched. Troubled, I spoke with my mother and other family members, trying to sort out the image I had seen in the *Post*. Life seemed so complicated. A lot of it failed to make sense; yet, my five-year-old self was determined to comprehend the emotions in the picture.

With the benefit of hindsight, I suppose my reading of the *Post* gave my parents some semblance of hope. They had spent years raising a child whose screaming at all hours of the night threatened their sanity and productivity. My love for food ensured that my mother was often in the kitchen, fielding phone calls from friends who were shocked to find out that, hours later, she was still in the same room in which the call had begun. Given my behavior in these early years, my parents could hardly be blamed if their deepest, darkest fear was that their son would grow up to be an overweight troublemaker whose inability to sit still would lead to incarceration.

As much as I loved to read the newspaper, the activity was not without peril. In early 1998, I came upon an odd story on the front page. Something about President Clinton having an affair. *What did that mean?* I wondered. *Why would the president do that and how did his wife feel?* Into the kitchen I strode, confident that my mother could put to rest my most nagging questions. Especially about the acts those two committed together.

When I opened my mouth, I doubt my mother could have anticipated her five-year-old son asking about the finer details of intimate acts. Yet there I was, trying to understand this complicated world that I found so intriguing. My mother, true to form, answered my questions calmly and accurately.

"Ew," I said, "That's disgusting!" *Why would anyone want to do that?* I wondered.

LONGING FOR HOME

No good deed goes unpunished.
—Unknown

As we returned from the storage unit to the man's home, I began to wonder what else may be in store.

When we arrived at the house, the man instructed us to remove everything from the truck and lay all of the items on his lawn. From there, he would sort through the objects and decide which would be placed in the garage and which would be put back into the truck. This process was time-consuming, causing further delays to our schedule. Once everything was finally sorted, the man inspected his garage, looking for any other items to put into the truck. More rearranging of various items took place. At some point, lunch was ordered, and the man paid the bill. Blake and I took a few slices of Papa John's Pizza and sat at the base of the lawn while the man and his wife sat just outside of their garage. Blake and

I, in our own private conversation, talked about the day and how long we expected the rest of the job to take. We talked about the impending start to the school year and caught up on all that had happened over the summer. While observing the man and woman from a distance, I noticed that they never seemed to touch each other in an affectionate way. They appeared to share little in common. The woman maintained an appearance that looked more appropriate for the 1950s than the 2000s, based on her hairstyle and clothing choices. She also looked significantly older than the man—possibly as much as twenty years older. It was hard to see what bonded the couple to each other at all.

After lunch, we continued loading the truck until it was nearly full. At this point, I still wasn't quite sure what would happen next. Blake and I had already been there much longer than anticipated, and I was ready to go home. The man had trouble making up his mind concerning which items should stay or go, changing course more than a few times in an effort to get it just right. The man indicated that another stop was in store, a friend's house "just down the road."

We had yet to leave the man's townhome when I received a phone call from my father. "I think it's time for you to leave," he said, his voice filled with concern. He quickly launched into a line of argument that sounded overprotective to my teenage ears. "You've been there too long," he said. He began asking where we were headed, how much longer the job would take. I tried to give him all of the information I had, which admittedly, was not much. My father was unsatisfied with my answers and continued urging me to return home.

As I listened to my father's words, I was torn about whether to leave or stay. "It's just five, ten minutes down the road," the man said calmly in the background. Based on this information, it felt as if the job was almost over. I had committed to completing the job, and it felt wrong to leave before it was completed. I was also intimidated by the man and was slightly worried about how he would respond if

I told him I needed to leave before finishing the job.

I told my father that I was staying and hung up the phone.

Soon after, we piled into the truck and left the house. Ten minutes into our trip, the man made a stop at Home Depot for trash bags. This detour increased my discomfort. "I'll be right back," the man said, leaving us in the truck while he entered the store. I looked at Blake and told him that this situation seemed to get stranger by the minute. I wondered if we should make a getaway, although I was unsure how we would do it. I thought about suggesting to Blake that we call our parents, but before I could say anything, the man returned. He placed his purchased items in the back of the truck and climbed into the driver's seat. I could not help but wonder why industrial bags were necessary. *What was it that we were going to be moving?* I wondered.

I attempted to engage the man once again. At one point, I asked him how he had met his wife. The man said that his wife had once been his landlord. He shared how they met, laughing as he declared he was the only tenant who had ever written her a check that did not bounce. The story ended there. Love at first sight became love at first check, I suppose.

After this aside, the truck was mostly silent. Uncertainty clouded the road ahead. The man occasionally commented that we were almost to the intended destination. I began to wonder if he was lost. We passed a sign that told us we had crossed into a new county whose name I did not recognize, and I started to feel very concerned. The possibility of escaping this situation seemed to grow less likely with each passing second. *How would I explain this to my parents?* I wondered.

Approximately 45 minutes later, the man made a sudden U-turn. We drove along a gravel road until he made a sharp right turn.

It felt like the longest 45 minutes of my life. Eventually, we arrived at a house at the top of a hill. The man steered the truck past the house and continued down the hill, turning this way and that until we reached a shed surrounded by trees. Blake and I jumped out of the truck to help the man back up the truck close to the shed. A middle-aged, blonde-haired woman appeared, walking down the hill toward us, followed by a gaggle of dogs. They were barking and clamoring at the sight of us, circling around the woman. She stood in place stoically, staring at the three of us.

The man stopped the truck and removed the key, causing the rumbling engine to cease. He and the woman greeted each other, talking for a few minutes before discussing plans to complete the work. "We have until nightfall," the man called out as he pushed the back door of the truck open.

Until nightfall? I thought. The job was supposed to end at 1 p.m. Now we were expected to work until nightfall?

I turned around and walked towards the truck. Maybe my father was right, after all. I searched for my backpack, looking for my phone until I was interrupted by the man asking me to assist with unpacking the truck.

As the man started to unload the contents of the truck, he stuck his hands deep into the boxes, selecting items that he wanted to return back to the house. "He's gonna help sell these on Amazon," the man said, pointing to me while he removed books that had failed to make it through his initial filtering process. Apparently, I was his online assistant. The job kept getting bigger, the duties exceeding the life of our verbal contract. The man then said something about planning a bonfire at the woman's house in the near future, to which Blake and I could bring our "girlfriends." My mind began to race, my pulse quickening. Something didn't feel right.

When will this end? I thought to myself.

I began mentally preparing for a long night ahead. It didn't look like I would be heading home anytime soon.

THE WORLD TURNS UPSIDE DOWN

There is nothing permanent except change.
—Heraclitus

The job got even bigger once the door of the shed was opened.

The woman's face changed at the sight of boxes, wood, art supplies, glass, and various other items piled in the shed. She mumbled something about how everything in the shed belonged to her ex-husband and pointed to a concrete slab nearby. She instructed us to "toss" every one of her ex-husband's possessions onto the concrete and stated that the garbage truck would come pick it all up later that week.

The man readily agreed that we would empty the shed. Blake and I walked up to the doorway of the shed where the woman ushered a flimsy cardboard box into my hands. "Toss it," she said.

I glanced into the loosely opened cardboard box and spotted books and hay. I hesitated for a moment and then, in one swift motion, tossed the box as the woman had instructed.

As soon as the box hit the concrete slab, a piercing sound assaulted my ears. It was higher than a hiss and louder than a scream. It sounded as if an explosion had occurred. I turned my head only to see a liquid flying through the air, coming straight toward me. I instinctively closed my eyes. I felt the liquid hit my face, neck, and arms, thick and foreign on my skin. My face in particular felt heavy under the weight of whatever it was. I was in shock, unable to process anything. Until the pain began.

My skin began to burn. It felt like my body was on fire as the fluid penetrated my skin. Images of bright orange flames entered my mind; it felt as if I had just walked into a fire. My heart raced. Panic washed over me. My eyes felt heavy, and I struggled to continue standing.

Blake rushed up to me and asked what was wrong. I attempted to speak, but all I could do was cry out in pain. The man wandered over and asked what was wrong. I couldn't answer, which prompted him to enlist Blake's help in lifting me onto the back of the truck. After they had laid me down, the man reached into the cooler nearby and retrieved a bottle of water. He unscrewed the cap and haphazardly poured water over my face. The liquid made its way across my face, bringing sweet relief with it.

Suddenly, the water stopped flowing and the pain returned. It felt like someone had lit a match and dropped it on my face.

Blake urged the man to call 911. The man resisted and told Blake to get back to work. Blake refused and continued to beg the man to call an ambulance.

Someone eventually called 911. I overheard the man describe my injuries to the 911 operator as "an acid burn." Suddenly I found myself removed from the truck and returned to a standing position as the man guided me up the hill. I stumbled forward, each step feeling heavier and more burdensome than the one before.

The pain was overwhelming. I leaned on the man and relied on him to get me up the hill. I tried to endure the pain by summoning images of streams of water, convincing myself that relief would return once we reached the top of the hill.

We finally reached the top of the hill. The 911 operator asked the man to identify the substance on my skin. He was unsure. "Where is this material? I need to go back and get it," he said to me. "Where is this stuff?"

"In the box," I said.

"Now you stay here. I'm gonna get some more water," he said, as he lowered me onto the ground and left the phone in my hands. Then he was gone, walking back down the hill and leaving me alone.

I looked around but could barely understand where I was. I did my best to put the phone to my ear.

"Sir, I am going to be giving some information to the ambulance," the operator said, "so if you could just stay on the line with me, I am not hanging up." The operator's voice was comforting, with a slight lilt and a Southern accent.

"Okay," I said shakily. My eyes remained closed. I couldn't hide my agony any longer, groaning as I attempted to control my pain.

"Okay, sweetie, we're here," the operator said.

"Yes," I said.

"One ambulance is on its way," she said.

"Uh-huh," I responded.

The knowledge that an ambulance was en route was comforting. I longed for the paramedics to arrive and ease my pain.

"About how much stuff splashed onto you?" the operator asked.

"I don't know," I said shakily. I kept pondering her question, trying to quantify the exact amount of liquid that had hit my skin. The pain continued and I began to wonder whether or not I would die.

"We were cleaning stuff out and I had a box," I said, my voice gaining strength with each word.

"And I put . . . I put it down and it . . . and it broke. I guess the can broke and it splashed and . . ." My voice trailed off. Feeling a wave of intense pain, my ability to continue speaking was derailed.

The 911 operator said, "Okay, okay, hold on."

"Yeah, yeah, yeah," I said in a strained voice, unable to summon the strength to utter anything else. A few seconds of silence fell over the call. In the intervening moments, I longed for the operator to tell me everything was going to be okay. I wished that she would tell me that this nightmare was about to end. I wanted to wake up, to rouse myself from this gut-wrenching dream. I wondered again if this was the end. "Do you want me to die on this hill?" I silently asked God.

A LOVE OF FOOD

There is no love sincerer than the love of food.
—George Bernard Shaw

My love for food began at an early age. My appetite often got me into trouble. Sunday nights were reserved for family dinner after church. Each week, we picked a new restaurant.

When our food would arrive at the table, I immediately devoured my meal. Unable to control myself, each french fry would disappear from my plate at rapid speed. One bite of a sandwich quickly turned into two or three, as if the temptation to gobble down my food was too great to withstand. Eating was a race against the clock. Pangs of hunger, no matter how slight, drove me to complete all meals as quickly as possible.

My lack of impulse control extended far beyond my own plate. My brother, Noah, nearly four years younger than me, was, by any standard, a slow eater. He carefully chewed each bite, ensuring that his plate almost always had more food than mine. One night at dinner, as my sweet, innocent brother sat taking bites of his sandwich, I surreptitiously snagged a few french fries on the edges of his plate. I had to carefully reach toward his plate to avoid drawing his attention and blowing my cover. My lack of self-control, coupled with my inability to pull off a successful french fry heist, was like kicking the hornet's nest of my brother's emotions.

"Mom, he ate my fries!" Noah yelled.

"Samuel, stop eating your brother's fries," my parents responded, threatening to make me change seats with them to increase the distance between me and my brother.

Later that night, hours after dinner, Noah asked, "Why did you take my fries?" befuddled by my behavior.

I didn't have an answer. I didn't know the answer. In those moments of hunger, it was as if my body kicked into an automatic response and I couldn't stop eating. Most nights, Noah didn't finish his meal anyway and gave me his leftovers. In my mind, I was simply speeding up the process by preemptively taking his food, thereby avoiding a situation where the family had to sit in the restaurant for hours, waiting for Noah to finish his food.

My lack of control came back to haunt me in other, unexpected ways. Extended family members, who did not like seeing any food go to waste, often placed pressure on me to complete the job. I became the designated vacuum cleaner of food, cleaning Noah's plate even when I was full. This occasionally led to painful consequences.

For example, one time I ate a large piece of cake at a family reunion. "You have a big appetite," my grandmother told me as she guided me toward a large piece of cake.

I ate the last bite of cake and instantly felt like I had made a grave mistake. My stomach began to rumble, growing louder with each episode. It did not take long for the rumbling to morph into aching—the kind of aching that might force me to the bathroom. I tried to take deep breaths to stave off the impending doom, but to no avail. I ran out of the hotel ballroom, sprinting toward the bathroom.

My father followed me and watched as I lost my dinner all over the beautiful red carpet of the hotel. A line of puke dotted the hallway, laid out with precision from one end of the hall to the other. My father ran to me and pushed me straight toward the elevator, trying to escape the group of hotel managers rapidly approaching from the other end of the hall.

After changing my clothes, we snuck back inside the hotel ballroom to rejoin our family.

At the end of the night, as we made our way back to our rooms, we saw that the housekeeping crew now filled the hall, addressing the stench and stained carpet. A manager stood in the center of the crew with a megaphone, asking all guests who happened to walk by, "Who did this? This carpet is brand new—who did this?"

I walked by with my father, who chuckled and muttered something about how I really knew how to leave an impression.

In the years following, my propensity for throwing up increased. It began to grate on my parents, especially when I ruined a rental car during a family trip to Texas and consequently forced my father to miss a visit to the zoo (one of his favorite places). Only years later did I begin to understand these unpleasant incidents. They consistently occurred after spending time with extended family. I will leave the analysis of that to a psychologist. Regardless, I learned that overeating became a way to contain my intense feelings, a way of stuffing my emotions deep inside, just like a piece of cake.

IF ONLY DAD WERE HERE

*I cannot think of any need in childhood as strong
as the need for a father's protection.*
—Sigmund Freud

"Okay, and is it your dad that is with you?" the 911 operator continued.

The question hit me hard. If only I had listened to my father when he had called hours before and urged me to leave the man's house. How did my father know that this situation would be dangerous?

As I tried to process the operator's question, I wished I could tell her that my father was there. He would know what to do.

But he wasn't. My father wasn't there, and I was completely and entirely alone.

"No," I answered. I felt guilty for ignoring my father's warnings and for putting myself in this situation.

Without missing a beat, the operator responded, "No, okay. So the man is going to go back and see if he can find out what it was?"

By this point, it felt like the man had been gone for several minutes, and I wondered if he would ever return. Or, if he did, what he would do or say. So much of how I had envisioned this day unfolding didn't happen. I turned my head while attempting to open my eyes, hoping to catch a glimpse of the man. *He couldn't have gone too far,* I thought.

But the man was nowhere to be found. It was quiet on the hill. The grass was unchanged, the leaves on the trees were still. I felt like I was burning alive, but the rest of the world existed as if nothing was wrong.

"Yes," I agreed with the operator that the man must have gone to find the substance. I hoped it was true.

"I heard the man say that you are having trouble with your eyes— did it get into your eyes?" the operator continued.

I attempted to open my eyes, but it felt like someone had placed heavy weights on top of them. "It might have, it might have," I said shakily. *Will I be blind?* I thought.

BURNING ALIVE

The real man smiles in trouble, gathers strength
from distress, and grows brave by reflection.
—Thomas Paine

As I waited for the man to return, my conversation with the 911 operator continued.

"It's on my lips," I told her.

"Are your lips bleeding?" she asked. "Has it done anything to your lips? Do they feel like they are burning?"

"Yeah, they feel very heavy," I said.

Silence again. With each second, my pain worsened. My lips began to feel heavier, and I worried that the substance had reached the inside of my mouth. I started to spit, trying to get rid of any traces of the substance in my mouth.

"Now, do you feel like anything is still burning on you?" she asked.

"Yeah, it kind of feels like my lips are kind of heavy," I said again. It was difficult to say anything else.

"You are having a little bit of trouble talking? Does it feel like your lips are swelling up?"

The skin on my face felt swollen, and my lips felt like they had doubled in size.

"They put some water on it and it felt better, but now it is starting to feel bad again," I said.

I couldn't stop thinking about water. I wanted to feel its cold touch cascading down my face. I hoped the man would appear with an endless supply of water. I remembered the cooler with water bottles that we packed earlier that day. *Why couldn't he bring those to me?* I wondered.

The 911 operator began to provide instructions about the water. It needed to be done in a specific way, "so that none of the chemicals run down any other part of your body," she explained.

"What I need you to let me know is if you end up having any trouble breathing, okay?" she continued. "Or if there is any problem with your tongue, if your tongue feels weird. The ambulance is on its way," she said. "You all are just a little ways out."

"Okay . . . okay," I muttered. With my eyes still closed, I tried to imagine the relief I would feel once the ambulance arrived.

I opened my eyes and saw the owner of the house standing nearby with her arms crossed, staring down at me. She looked imposing now, her face unmoved as she watched me in silence.

Eventually, she asked if baking soda would help my face. I remember holding the phone out at one point offering the woman a chance to speak to the 911 operator directly. She refused, shaking her head in response.

"Should, uh, we put baking soda on it?" I asked the 911 operator.

"Um, probably not," the operator said. "All the information that I show says that the best thing to do is to flush it with a lot of cold, ya know, cool running water."

I tried to relay this message to the woman.

At some point, I remember the woman walking back towards her house and returning with a bucket. She said that the bucket was full of warm water. The 911 operator continued her phone instructions as if on cue: "Just not warm water, ya know, you don't want anything hot and you want to try to not let that water touch any other part of your body that doesn't already have chemical on it, okay?"

I did my best to relay this message to the woman. Before I knew it, she was gone. I wondered if she would return with cold water. *Where had the man gone?*

I closed my eyes once again, trying to fight the pain. "Oh, God," I said, followed by repeated groans.

My breathing became more labored. I had trouble getting the air my lungs needed. I felt like I was in the middle of a desert trying to navigate without knowing what lay ahead. I didn't know how much longer I could do this. I felt like I was going to faint.

I wanted to close my eyes and fall asleep. I needed to escape the pain. I kept praying, asking God to give me strength.

The 911 operator suddenly said, "Was he able to get some more water?"

"Yeah, he's coming with it," I replied, as I watched him walking up the hill.

Then I heard the sirens. It was the sweetest sound I had ever heard.

"Okay, well you actually have three ambulances coming to you because of where your location is, so you have them coming from a couple different directions," the operator said.

"Oh, thank God," I said, crying in pain.

Soon after, the man and Blake finally appeared with water. The man asked how the water should be applied and I told him.

"Yeah, just so it doesn't get back into your eyes, ya know what I mean? If you've got it in your hair then you don't want to pour it over top of your head and let it drain into your eyes, okay? You want to keep it away," she said.

The man instructed Blake to get down on his hands and knees. Then I moved myself onto Blake's back, crying out in pain during the jostling and movement. As soon as I was in place, the man began pouring water over my face.

The cool liquid felt soothing, lessening my pain. The water changed my perspective. Perhaps everything would be okay.

But then, the flow of water came to an abrupt halt. Before I could ask for more, everything began to get blurry. Someone moved me from Blake's back to the ground again. Then they left, and I was alone again. The pain came roaring back. My body felt like it was getting smaller.

When the ambulance arrived, a group of men spilled out, racing toward me. They lifted me onto a stretcher and carried me toward the ambulance. The paramedics shouted instructions to each other, coordinating next steps as they carefully placed me down.

Oh God, what have I done? I thought to myself as they lifted me into the ambulance.

It was in that moment in the ambulance when I remember being struck by the beauty of the trees. I wondered if that was the last time I would see trees.

HELP HAS ARRIVED

What a strange illusion it is to suppose that beauty is goodness.
—Leo Tolstoy, *Anna Karenina*

"Does it hurt like hell?" one of the paramedics asked me in the ambulance.

"Yes," I said.

My body was riddled with pain. The paramedics hovered around me, frantically attempting to assess my current state. At some point, one of them asked if I had seen what had burned me. "No," I responded. Before we departed, I watched as a few paramedics, along with a few law enforcement officers, approached the woman. Within a few minutes, they had returned. Based on comments made by the paramedics, I gleaned that the authorities had asked the woman to hand over the box, and she had refused. I found this utterly confusing. *What was it that she was trying to hide?* I wondered.

With that, we were off toward our intended destination.

"We need to get water in your eyes," one of the paramedics told me. He pulled a table of medical supplies toward him while the other paramedics moved about the ambulance and picked up a device that looked like the water spout at a dentist's office. He began to flush my eyes with water, pausing every so often. This felt good on my eyes, but the rest of my face and body still felt like they were burning with pain. I wanted the water to leak out of my eyes and flow onto the rest of my face, but I wondered if the paramedics were refraining from doing so for a reason, which kept me from making such a request. Occasionally a drop or two did splash onto my face, and it felt soothing.

The paramedic flushing my eyes hovered just above my body, a few inches from my face. I could see his eyes carefully watching me, darting back and forth as he assessed my injuries. It seemed like he couldn't look away. I detected almost a tinge of fascination in his face regarding my injuries.

"Does it hurt like hell?" he asked again.

He kept repeating that question over and over. Each time, I said the same thing. "Yes."

Where was Blake? I wondered. I thought I heard him mention something about following the ambulance. *Would he be at the hospital when I got there?* I worried something bad would happen to him, too. They only had room for me in the ambulance, but I'd wished they had allowed him to ride along.

The pain was overwhelming. I kept praying, asking God to take it away. I wanted to hear God's voice. I wanted him to appear suddenly and rescue me.

"This is ambulance number . . . calling in for permission to . . ." the paramedic with the radio said.

I was having trouble understanding all the words exchanged

between the operator and the responder on the line. The siren blared. The vehicle hummed noisily as we sped along the highway. The other paramedics held frenzied conversations. All of this drowned out the radio in a chaotic blur. I heard something about morphine.

The paramedic who had been flushing my eyes with water stopped and another paramedic approached me with a needle. He quickly injected my shoulder with the needle.

A few minutes went by and my pain level felt worse than before. "I'm still in pain," I said. Two of the men glanced at each other and shrugged. "Hang in there until we get to the hospital," one said.

Meanwhile, I wasn't sure I could make it to the hospital. The pain was excruciating. I felt myself getting weak. The pain was taking over my ability to control my body.

We took a quick turn and slowed to a halt. Someone opened the door of the ambulance and the paramedics lifted me to the ground. A team of nurses hovered around me, snapping the rails of the stretcher in place as they grabbed a spot along the sides, wheeling me into the building.

We entered a large, dark room where I was stripped, the nurses piling around, cutting off each article of clothing from my body.

I didn't know what was happening. They thrust my naked body onto a giant table and one nurse came barreling toward me with an oversized showerhead.

Suddenly I felt cool water washing over my skin. It was the sweetest feeling I've ever experienced. My pain evaporated. I took a deep breath for the first time since the cardboard box exploded. As the water cascaded down my skin, the nurses directed the showerhead closer to my face. After a few moments, in one swift movement, I was lifted by the team of nurses and placed onto a stretcher.

OUT COMES THE MIRROR

Everyone who got where he is has had to begin where he was.
—Robert Louis Stevenson

I was laying on the stretcher as the team of nurses wheeled me through the hospital. Along the way, a doctor joined the medical entourage. He asked a few questions, taking a look as he walked to assess my injuries. He asked what burned me. I told him I didn't know. He looked frustrated. I tried to tell him what happened, but he walked away mid-sentence with a scoff. I felt like I had done something wrong.

Eventually, we arrived at a large space—not quite a room, but more like an open area. Nurses entered and exited, performing various tasks—placing an IV in my arm, injecting pain medications. One nurse injected me with a needle and I grimaced. "You are going to feel better," she said.

Minutes later, she was right. The pain subsided and the burning sensation lessened. The flame, for now, was extinguished.

Then, the nurses began to run a battery of tests as I continued to lay on the mobile hospital bed, including an x-ray, as well as an inspection of my eyelids, lips, and mouth. It was determined that I had suffered first-, second- and third-degree burns to my face, neck, ears, and arms. One nurse asked, "What was it that spilled on you?" I still didn't know the answer. Someone else asked the question again. Each time I said I didn't know members of the medical staff furrowed their brows, looking at me quizzically. Some even gasped.

Another nurse asked, "Why didn't you bring the box to the hospital?" I tried to explain what happened: that I didn't have the opportunity to go search for the box as my body was burning. They expressed a desire to test the substance, suggesting it might help with my treatment. All I could do was describe what it felt like in an effort to give them the information they needed. Regardless, they still kept asking for the box.

The medical staff concluded their work and determined that I had no internal damage. I was informed of how lucky I was; that if I had ingested the substance, my esophagus and possibly other organs could have suffered damage. I shuddered at the thought of all that could have gone wrong.

Soon after, Blake walked into the room. "How are you feeling?" he asked, his eyes scanning my face. He asked if I had been burned anywhere other than my face, and I showed him the marks on my arms. He looked relieved that the damage wasn't greater and stood up straighter as if a weight had fallen off his shoulders.

He made a joke about my experience in the chemical shower, saying how lucky I was that female nurses had given me a "sponge bath." Of course, I knew there had been no sponges involved, but his imagination was getting the best of him. I had not enjoyed the experience at all, feeling like a naked animal getting my clothes ripped off.

I asked if anything had happened to him. He said that the substance had blown holes through the top of his white t-shirt, but he had no injuries. I was relieved and grateful to know that he had been spared.

Soon after, the man who had hired me for the job entered the room. Blake shuffled closer toward me and away from the man. Blake's demeanor changed as soon as he saw the man and he clenched the rails of my hospital bed. Within seconds, the man began to speak.

"She lent me her car. Wasn't that nice of her?" he said.

A little confused as to whom he was referring, he went on to tell me that the woman's kindness allowed him to arrive at the hospital faster than he would have been able to drive the jam-packed U-Haul. He told me he had been driving well past the speed limit. As he shared this information, he looked over at Blake to confirm his account, who nodded in response.

I pieced the story together while listening. Apparently, the woman who owned the house had lent her vehicle to the man. I wondered why she didn't come with them to the hospital. I still didn't know what the relationship between the man and woman entailed.

Then the man mumbled something, saying that the liquid substance was sulfuric acid. He said it had been in a Mason jar at the bottom of the cardboard box underneath the books and hay. He said the jar had been labeled, "Sulfuric acid 1%."

"Did it get in your eyes?" the man asked me.

I told him that my eyesight was still intact and he exhaled loudly.

"Thank God!" he said. "Have you seen yourself yet?" he asked while peering down at me.

"No," I said.

A nurse standing nearby asked if I wanted to see myself in the mirror. I wasn't sure if I wanted to see myself. Before I could respond, the nurse tossed a mirror into my lap and said, "Here, take a look."

I grasped the mirror and braced myself before taking a look at my face. I held it in front of me and inspected my reflection. My cheeks were covered with large black and green stains extending toward the lower part of my face. I had marks on my neck, which looked as if I had been clawed by an animal. I barely recognized myself. My face looked like it had been caked in mud, with brown and black stains covering it. I shuddered, then pushed the mirror away from my face as far as I could.

Samuel Moore-Sobel

TIME TO FLY AWAY

You haven't seen a tree until you've
seen its shadow from the sky.
—Amelia Earhart

"I'm going to pay you one hundred fifty dollars rather than one hundred twenty-five dollars," the man told me, "even though you didn't finish the job."

He pushed an envelope into my hands. I looked down at the envelope and could see the label with the hospital's address on the front. Then the man turned to Blake and asked him to return to the woman's house so he could finish the job. Blake recoiled, stepping backward slightly as the man urged him to leave. Blake made it clear that he wanted to stay with me.

"Well, at least you have your eyes," the man said to me. The more he talked, the more uncomfortable I felt. I averted my eyes, trying to distance myself from the man. I tried to sink further down into my bed. The nurses sensed my distress and asked the man to leave.

Once the man walked out, Blake started talking about his plans for the rest of the summer. He was excited to have extra cash and was trying to decide what items he was going to purchase. Blake also said he told my parents what had happened. He said that at the scene of the accident, he had found my cell phone and called them as soon as he had reception. He called my dad first and told him that I had been in an accident. My dad dropped the phone to the floor. Blake, hearing silence on the other end, thought they had been disconnected. "Hello?" he said repeatedly, until my father finally returned the phone to his ear and began to speak.

At some point, a nurse appeared holding a bag of my belongings. Nike shoes, socks, shorts, and a t-shirt. "Do you want these?" he asked, before cautioning that additional chemicals might be on the clothing. I saw no need to keep the items. He offered to dispose of all contents in the bag, and I agreed.

It wasn't long before an influx of medical staff came into the room. They said that I would be transported by helicopter to Children's Hospital in Washington, D.C. which had more experience with burn survivors. A team of paramedics moved my body onto a stretcher and strapped me onto it. In the flurry of activity and motion, I felt lost and uncertain about what was going on. I hoped my mother would arrive at the hospital before I left on the helicopter.

When I was a child, whenever I felt sad, anxious, or overwhelmed, I used to crawl into bed with my mom and rest my head on her chest. She would caress my hair and softly remind me that "It's going to be okay." I became accustomed to this comforting phrase. I would often wait until she said those words before crawling back to my own room for the night.

What I learned from her words was that life would never unfold exactly the way I planned, but no matter what happened, she would be there to tell me she loved me and that I had the strength and courage to face whatever came my way.

Moments before I was set to depart by helicopter, my mother arrived. From the moment she laid eyes on me, I knew she saw my fear. I looked into her eyes. *Was she startled by how I looked?* I wondered. To the contrary, her eyes were full of strength, with a determination to reach me before I was wheeled away. "I love you," she said, before carefully kissing the top of my head. "I'll meet you at the hospital. It's going to be okay." With that, our short visit was over, and the para-medics wheeled me toward the helipad.

Strong winds greeted me on the tarmac. As we inched closer to the helicopter, the wind from the rotor blades felt good on my face. I felt the sun on my skin as we inched closer; the deafening noise of the helicopter was disorientating.

The helicopter was cramped and my stretcher took up most of the area. One man positioned himself nearby and a similarly-clad fellow jumped aboard. They shouted instructions to one another, readying the cabin for takeoff.

I longed to catch a glimpse of my mother but could not see out the window. I felt uneasy embarking on my first helicopter ride with complete strangers. "Let me know if you feel nauseous," the medic told me before we got into the air. I placed my head on the pillow, bracing myself for a bumpy ride.

I kept quiet, grateful that my pain was still minimal. I started to feel nauseated. My throat tensed up, and I thought I was about to vomit. I tried to tell the medic, but no sound came out of my mouth. I felt trapped, the painkillers and shock preventing me from speaking. Luckily, the medic noticed.

"I told you to let me know when you felt nauseous!" he said.

He inserted something in my IV, and I immediately felt better. My eyes closed, and I began to fall in and out of sleep.

Suddenly, the medic shouted, "Look down! There is the Washington Monument!"

I briefly lifted my head to catch a glimpse of the view. It was beautiful and nearly close enough to touch as we flew by. I saw the green grass below and the American flags at the base of the monument. I closed my eyes and fell back onto the pillow, hoping I would get the chance to see the monument again under better circumstances.

Moments later, we arrived at Children's Hospital. The medics lifted me from the helicopter to the ground. The wind swirled around me, providing brief relief. The view of the city was breathtaking, offering hope in the midst of intense pain.

I marveled at the circumstances in which I found myself as the medical team guided me through the open, glass doors. Met by hospital staff upon our arrival, I was gently guided toward a room down a large corridor. After I had been safely placed in the room, I was informed that a nurse would be by to check on me shortly before everyone shuffled out. A sense of quiet fell over the room, and I was left alone for the first time after hours of near constant activity.

I looked around the white, sterile room. It seemed larger now that everyone was gone. I felt lonely sitting in that large room by myself. I wanted my parents to arrive. My eyes started to feel heavy. As determined as I was to stay awake until my parents arrived, my strength was no match for the medication in my veins. I fell into a deep sleep, catching a few minutes of rest before the journey continued.

HOW DO I LOOK?

I've never seen a smiling face that was not beautiful.
—Unknown

When I woke up, my friend Michael was standing in the doorway with tears streaming down his face. At first, I was confused. *How did he know I was here?* I wondered.

Michael, a bearded fellow known for his penchant for hats, stood still as he watched me. Sadness filled his eyes, and his lips contorted as tears streamed down his face. I looked back at him. His wife, Miriam, pulled him out of view. I heard her whispering to him in the hallway. Miriam emerged soon after and made her way toward my bed.

I was frightened by Michael's reaction to my injuries. I wanted to know the extent of the damage from their point of view. *Does my face look worse than it did a few hours ago?* I wondered.

Miriam spoke soothing, gentle words. She reached for my hand

and said that everything was going to be okay. She said it with confidence, while speaking softly—her words effectively distracted me from her husband's display of emotion just moments before. Michael re-entered the room, this time without tears.

"How do I look?" I asked Miriam, watching her reaction. She held my hand and squeezed tightly.

"I am looking on the inside, not the outside," she said.

I repeated my question, unsatisfied with her answer.

"I am looking on the inside, not the outside," she said once again, her voice cracking a bit. She rubbed her hand up and down my arm, reassuring me that she was not focused on my appearance.

Eventually, my father arrived. He stood at the edge of the room, a look of horror on his face as his gaze met mine. He erupted into tears; within seconds, Michael had pulled my father out of the room. I could hear them as they spoke in the hallway, shrouded in hushed tones, with Michael urging my father to remain strong.

Soon after, my mother appeared. Just as before, she looked unfazed by my appearance, reaching for my hand, reassuring me. She asked how I was feeling and how the helicopter ride was. She spoke with Miriam and thanked her for coming to the hospital. She smiled and spoke as she normally did. Her presence was soothing and helped me feel more comfortable. I sat up, talking to my mother as we waited for the doctor.

Meanwhile, nurses shuffled in and out of the room, informing us that hospital staff was preparing a room for my overnight stay. They asked me to describe my pain levels using a chart from zero to ten. Thankfully, my pain was low, although my discomfort was high. My skin felt weighty and not my own, and my grogginess grew as the afternoon faded to evening.

Finally, I was wheeled into a large room with a couch in the corner for my parents to occupy. The room was replete with a bathroom, and the walls were painted with an array of colors, likely intended to be child-friendly. This was Children's Hospital, after all. I felt a bit out of place as my large frame and teenaged status placed me closer to adulthood than childhood.

My mother and I settled in for the night. Unable to sleep, I recounted pieces of the day, attempting to string together the events of the past few hours. "He said his friend's house was 'just down the road,'" I said. I realized I was the only one talking and my mother was silent. I looked over at her, noticing that she kept checking her phone. She was surprised that my father had not yet returned.

Eventually, he did return. When he walked through the door, his shoulders slumped. He looked serious and started talking about his trip home. After gathering what he needed, he drove the few blocks to the man's house. It was well past 1 a.m. when my father sat in his SUV, watching the man carry boxes from his lawn into his garage. As my father watched, he thought about confronting the man. My father felt his fury toward the man grow with each passing moment. *He almost killed my son,* I imagined my father thinking in that moment. Exercising great self-control, he continued to sit in the car.

My father recounted his experience as my mother and I listened with wide eyes. "I didn't want to go to jail," he said quietly, explaining that he eventually left the scene.

A BRIEF LESSON ON SULFURIC ACID

Only the educated are free.
—Epictetus

Sulfuric acid is one of the most dangerous chemical compounds in the world. It is often used in the production of fertilizers, batteries, cleaning products, paints, and explosives.[1] A "colorless oily liquid,"[2] the Occupational Safety and Health Administration (OSHA) has strict guidelines concerning its storage and use.

Sulfuric acid is so dangerous that the Department of Labor recommends "employees should be provided with and required to use impervious clothing, gloves, face shields (eight-inch minimum), and

---

[1] Sulfuric acid. (2004, September 16). Retrieved from https://pubchem.ncbi.nlm.nih. gov/compound/Sulfuric-acid.
[2] Ibid.

other appropriate protective clothing necessary to prevent any possibility of skin contact with liquid sulfuric acid . . ."[3] Additionally, it is recommended that workers wear safety goggles and have access to a fountain to wash their eyes or shower their bodies in the case of an emergency.[4]

Chemical burns such as those from sulfuric acid are just as serious, if not more so, than burns from fire. Sulfuric acid is "corrosive," which "means it can cause severe burns and tissue damage when it comes into contact with the skin or mucous membranes."[5] A person can be exposed to sulfuric acid "if it is inhaled," "comes in contact with the eyes or skin," or if it is "swallowed."[6] When it comes to contact with sulfuric acid, "extensive damage to the mouth, throat, eyes, lungs, esophagus, nose, and stomach is possible."[7]

In the United States, between the years of 1999 and 2013, "chemical burn injuries accounted for approximately 3 percent of all burn injuries," according to a report of recorded hospital cases involving burn injury patients.[8] Some of those cases are the result of sulfuric acid used as a weapon in criminal activity. For example, in 2008, British model Katie Piper suffered severe burns when her ex-boyfriend hired someone to "throw sulfuric acid into her face."[9] In 2010,

---

[3] Occupational Health Guideline for Sulfuric Acid. (n.d.). Retrieved from https://www.cdc.gov/niosh/docs/81-123/pdfs/0577.pdf.

[4] Ibid.

[5] Heller, J. (2018, June 24). Sulfuric acid poisoning: Medline Plus Medical Encyclopedia. Retrieved from https://medlineplus.gov/ency/article/002492.htm.

[6] Occupational Health Guideline for Sulfuric Acid. (n.d.). Retrieved from https://www.cdc.gov/niosh/docs/81-123/pdfs/0577.pdf.

[7] Heller, J. (2018, June 24). Sulfuric acid poisoning: Medline Plus Medical Encyclopedia. Retrieved from https://medlineplus.gov/ency/article/002492.htm.

[8] Hall, A. H., (2018, September 18). Acute chemical skin injuries in the United States: a review. Retrieved from https://www.tandfonline.com/doi/full/10.1080/10408444.2018.1493085.

[9] Newton, J. (2019, October 10). What happened to Katie Piper and what did she look like before the acid attack? Retrieved from https://www.thesun.co.uk/tvandshowbiz/3159251/katie-piper-acid-attack-survivor-model-husband-fighting-crime/.

a woman claimed to have been injured by an acid attack but had actually injured herself;[10] and, in 2013, the director of the Moscow Ballet, Sergei Filin, was attacked with sulfuric acid and was left "partially blinded."[11]

As alarming as these statistics are, they only illuminate part of the reality. They cannot replace the stories of individuals all across the world who have experienced firsthand the horror of a burn injury. The emotional repercussions of the burns transcend the physical pain; quite literally, the burn survivor's skin is forever changed. Since the accident, I have not felt comfortable in my own skin. My face doesn't feel like my own. I feel like foreign objects are clinging to me and each time I touch my scars, it feels like I am touching rubber. These feelings, along with the alterations in physical appearance, have long-lasting effects. Each burn survivor's story is unique, but one truth remains: what has been lost can never fully be regained.

[10] Tomlinson, S. (2011, March 2). Bethany Storro of Vancouver, who burned her face with acid, faces trial in May. Retrieved from https://www.oregonlive.com/clark-county/2011/03/trial_for_vancouver_wash_resident_bethany_storro_who_burned_her_own_face_with_drain_cleaner_postpone.html.

[11] Kennedy, M. (2016, November 3). Bolshoi Dancer Jailed For Acid Attack Reportedly Returns For Practice. Retrieved from https://www.npr.org/sections/thetwo-way/2016/11/03/500567324/bolshoi-dancer-jailed-for-acid-attack-reportedly-returns-for-practice.

SEEING IT ALL

Innocence, once lost, can never be regained.
Darkness, once gazed upon, can never be lost.
—John Milton

My first surgery after the accident lasted for hours longer than the doctors expected, as the medical staff was inexperienced with chemical burns. During surgery, the doctors were so unsure of how to proceed that they called colleagues at a nearby hospital for support over the phone.

It was a debridement surgery, an operation that cleans the wounds by scraping off dead skin to prevent the patient from contracting an infection. It scared me that the surgery took so much longer than anticipated, which planted the seeds of my fears related to anesthesia and surgery.

While I was in surgery, an ophthalmologist evaluated my eyes. To her surprise, she did not discover any damage. "I have no explanation for you as to why he can see," she told my parents. "From the condition of his eyelids, he should be blind."

A meeting with medical staff later that morning didn't give us many answers about a plan for treatment. "This type of injury is extremely rare," one medical professional said. Others echoed this sentiment. They were concerned about my left ear—it was covered in black marks that failed to lift after surgery. A few staff members suggested that the damage done to my ear might create hearing problems for me in the future.

Overall, the hospital staff said that I would heal in time. "You won't even be able to tell anything happened in a year," one doctor said.

We were told to be vigilant about signs of infection. If swelling occurred, we were to immediately return to the hospital. As a preventative measure, I was told to keep my face moist with bacitracin and to avoid direct contact with sunlight.

Armed with those instructions, we were told I would be discharged shortly. "There's nothing more we can do," a nurse told us.

Within twenty-four hours, my stay in the hospital came to a close.

On the long car ride back, we were left to ponder the implications of returning home. I felt hopeful, since the medical staff seemed optimistic about my recovery. But the road ahead still appeared daunting. Since my case was so rare, it already seemed difficult to find resources or information about healing. I felt like I was stuck in a dark, locked room.

The prospect of returning home raised my spirits, but I was concerned about my sister and brother seeing my face for the first time. I remembered Michael and Miriam's tears in reaction to my face. *How would my siblings respond to the sight of me?*

I looked around my neighborhood. It looked just as quiet and peaceful as it was when I left it yesterday. Everything was the same even though my life had dramatically changed.

I went inside the house. My seven-year-old sister was sitting in the loft playing computer games. Her eyes met mine. The moment she saw me, the color drained from her face. She looked as if she had seen a ghost. I saw pain, anguish, and fear wash over her. She froze, standing completely still for a few seconds without uttering a sound. Then she ran down the stairs with tears streaming across her face.

Her look hit me. It was as if she had seen someone die. It was as if her invincible older brother, whose job it was to protect her from the outside world, had been unable to protect himself. She knew then what took me far longer to learn—nothing would ever be the same again.

WILL JUSTICE BE SERVED?

It is better to suffer injustice than to commit it.
—Socrates

During my brief stay at the hospital, my parents made calls to investigate whether what happened to me involved any crimes. First, they called the police department located in the county where my injuries had occurred. My parents shared what had happened, telling the officer on duty that their son had been transported out of the county without their permission. They also described how the sulfuric acid was stored—precariously and dangerously. In response, the officer told my parents there was nothing he could do. He advised them to call back the next day when someone else might be able to assist. My parents also contacted our local sheriff's office to share the story once again. That office said to call back the next day in order to speak with a risk officer.

Mystery still enshrouded the true purpose of the sulfuric acid. At some point, either by the man or the authorities, it was revealed that the woman was claiming the substance belonged to her ex-husband. His alleged use of the sulfuric acid was for "metal etching," although no further details were proffered.

The next day, my parents made more phone calls to the police departments. Both departments informed my parents that no laws had been broken. My parents took my case all the way to the commonwealth attorney's office who also said that there was no evidence of state law violations. He did, however, suggest that my parents contact the fire marshal, since they could judge whether or not the manner in which the sulfuric acid had been stored violated code.

Upon further investigation, my parents learned that the county where the accident occurred did not have a fire marshal—at all. Without a fire marshal, residents were allowed to store chemicals in any manner without breaking the law.

A deputy sheriff in our home county advised my parents to contact OSHA. He thought that hiring a minor for a job which resulted in an injury might have violated certain OSHA regulations. OSHA agreed to take the case, engaging in a long investigation that involved interviewing myself, my parents, Blake, and others.

In the end, their efforts returned nothing. The investigators determined that the way in which I had obtained the job precluded the man from any charges, as well as the woman whose shed housed the acid. Nothing could be done.

My parents and I felt frustrated by this outcome. With no one left to contact, it felt as if all levels of government—local, state, and federal—had delivered a resounding verdict. This accident was entirely my fault, or, at the very least, the man and woman shouldered no culpability for what had occurred.

NO ESCAPE

Memory . . . is the diary that we all carry about with us.
—Oscar Wilde

My mother prided herself on her excellent memory. My father, forever her opposite, seemed unable to remember most things, from the important to the mundane. Sometimes this was a source of strife at home. "Those who do not know their history are doomed to repeat it," my mother would say, quoting the words of George Santayana.

Memory was an important part of my childhood. I built my memory skills in part through my obsession with American history and the presidency. By the age of eight, I could recite the complete list of United States presidents from beginning to end, which became a crowd-pleaser at family gatherings and dinner parties. I stored random facts in my brain, devouring book after book in order to learn more about the tales of great men, gleaning lessons from their own life paths. I went against the grain as a middle school student when I elected to bring a book about John Adams to sleep-away camp, much to the shock of my fellow campers and counselors.

I was taught that memory was a skill and gift to be treasured. I cultivated it enthusiastically. Memories shape and inform our own identities. Memories remind us who we are and who came before us. As such, I always prided myself on my ability to remember, believing I had a special skill that set me apart. My memory was a source of great joy—until the day I learned that memories could haunt.

In the days following the accident, I longed to itch every part of my face. I watched as my scars went from black and green to brown before hardening into a bright red. So disgusted was I by my new appearance that I took great pains to assiduously avoid looking in the mirror. As the new skin grew, I longed to scratch the itch, but the doctors warned against indulging such desires. In order to cope, I spent hours sitting on the couch in front of a tiny gray fan, the blades whirling on their highest setting. The cool breeze on my face helped to ease the itching, but nothing I tried ever fully eradicated my need to scratch.

A few days after the accident, I stood in the shower for the first time. Without much thought, I turned the showerhead towards hot water, eager to feel clean after being unable to shower. The warm water felt so good cascading down my body as the soap washed off, spinning around the drain. The warm water provided relief to my weary body. I placed my face directly under the showerhead and imagined for a moment that the water was washing away the ugly scars on my face. It was the most peaceful sensation.

Until suddenly it wasn't. The water felt heavy on my skin. The steam, rising from the warm water below, started to feel like it was burning my body. A drop of water entered my mouth and it tasted like tar. I began to spit it out. My face felt like it was on fire, the hot water boring holes into my skin. My head began to spin and it felt like I was experiencing the accident all over again. Fear gripped me, along with a sense of imminent danger. I panicked and moved to turn off the silver showerhead as quickly as I could. I reached for a towel, upset that even a peaceful shower turned into reliving unwanted memories—memories that were preserved, no matter how much I wanted to forget.

GRASPING AT STRAWS

Courage is not having the strength to go on; it is
going on when you don't have the strength.
—Theodore Roosevelt

Days after the accident, a team of medical professionals stood around me poking and prodding as I sat on the examination table in the center of the room. My father held a list of prepared questions in his hands. Holding the piece of paper with a loose grip, he fired away.

"How long will it take to recover?" my father asked.

"Oh, it is hard to say, but it should be healed in no more than a year," one medical professional said.

"What procedures will he need in the future?"

"Oh, we really don't know," someone replied. "We will refer you to a plastic surgeon to get those questions answered."

"What kind of foods should he eat?" my father asked.

"Fatty foods are good for the skin, so eat a lot of meat and potatoes," another advised.

My mother, a lover of organic products and proponent of alternative medicine, pushed for recommendations regarding alternative approaches. "Are there any other vitamins or alternative solutions to help Samuel heal?" she asked.

"No," someone said.

As the appointment came to a close, a doctor gave some last-minute advice. "Keep applying Aquaphor to your face."

Aquaphor had been my constant over the last few days. Determined to heal, I religiously applied this sticky substance to my face. It felt as if it invaded my skin without ever dissolving. No matter how much Aquaphor I applied, my skin still felt as dry as a desert.

Six days after the accident, I detected an increase in swelling around the scar on my right hand. I asked my father for his opinion. Standing in my parents' master bathroom, he examined the scar. Pulling my hand up closer to the light, he tried his best to judge whether or not I had contracted an infection. After a few minutes, he had made his determination.

"Yep, it's time to go," he said.

Then we were off, driving nearly an hour to Children's Hospital in Washington, D.C. I could barely keep my eyes off of my swollen right hand, throbbing endlessly as we pushed on towards our destination. The ride was quiet. *What if my hand was infected?* I wondered.

At the hospital, we checked in with a nurse at the entrance. From the looks of the full waiting room, it appeared that it would be hours before I could see a doctor.

Eventually, the nurse ushered us out of the noisy waiting room, veering straight back through the large double doors leading toward the patient rooms. The nurse examined my burn sites, awkwardly shifting her eyes back and forth, as if unsure of how best to look at my face and arms. "The doctor will be in shortly," the nurse said.

I sat quietly on the bed in the middle of the open room, a flimsy curtain separating one patient from another just a few feet away. Finally, a nurse entered the room. "I was reading your file, and your story is amazing!" she said. She asked a few follow-up questions, and my parents offered additional details, outlining the last week while I sat silently on the bed. Just seconds into the story, the nurse's face looked alarmed.

"You really should have been hurt much worse. And you weren't!" she said heartily. "You are very blessed!" I smiled reticently, unsure how to respond.

Moments later, the doctor appeared. Young and lean, she immediately took charge, lowering her head in an effort to get a closer look at my right hand. After a few minutes of inspection, she asked me to clench my fist, then unclench, then another clench while grabbing onto her hand at the same time.

After a few reps, she appeared satisfied by how my hand was responding. "Oh yeah, you are fine, no infection," she assured me.

Relieved, I returned my hand to my side, thankful that our fears of infection were unfounded.

"Just remember to keep applying bacitracin," the doctor said. "Do you need any more?"

"Yeah, that would be great," my dad said, even though we had a healthy supply back at home. The doctor said she would be right back, disappearing to locate more packets of bacitracin. At least the long trip will be worth something—a few packets of an over-the-counter moisturizer that could have been purchased at the nearby CVS for a few dollars.

She returned moments later, her arms filled with packets that looked similar to hand wipes. My father held out his arms, ready to receive the bundle of bacitracin from the doctor. Before we went our separate ways, she offered a few parting words. "You are so lucky," she said.

As I walked through the hospital, I pondered her words. I caught a glimpse of my father behind me, his arms filled with those packets of bacitracin. I didn't feel lucky.

WHIPLASH

Conceit spoils the finest genius.
— Louisa May Alcott, *Little Women*

I did not begin school on Tuesday, September 8, along with the rest of my class. Per doctor's orders, I remained at home to avoid infection. I didn't know how long I would be confined to the house. As the days went by, I began to feel like I would never return to school.

About a month after the accident, my long-awaited appointment with the plastic surgeon finally arrived. I felt hopeful as my parents and I made our return trip to Children's Hospital, as the promise of receiving answers from the surgeon generated much excitement. Friends and family had been lauding the skill of plastic surgeons, saying that they could correct any imperfections. The surgeon was eminently qualified, with years of experience, along with a teaching gig at George Washington University on his resume.

By this point, the scars had begun to take permanent shape. The most noticeable was the scar under my nose—a large, red line—right where my mustache used to grow. This was the most troublesome scar, the one most in need of revision.

The scar directly under my chin looked as if an ice-cream scoop extracted a giant gob of skin from my face. It ran down the side of my neck with lines that looked as if they belonged to an octopus, large tentacles wrapping around my neck as if choking anything that dared to cross this rugged scar's path. A lined scar across the left side of my neck looked as if a cat had stuck its claws deep into my skin and ran them across my face. A few extraneous scars marked my arms, the most noticeable in the shape of a starfish on the top corner of my right hand. Scars lined the left side of my right forearm, resembling tiny, bright red bullet holes.

Upon our arrival, we sat in the waiting room at Children's for what felt like an eternity, glancing at the same magazines from weeks before, anxiously awaiting the appointment. A nurse finally called my name and led us back into a similar room to the ones I remembered from my earlier stay. After repeated visits, the rooms were beginning to blend together. They all contained the same sterile smell and the same sink filled with utensils. A nurse entered, inquiring as to the reason for our visit. My mind started racing, my mouth refused to move. I felt entirely paralyzed, unable to answer the question. I looked at my mother, and she jumped in, detailing my injuries for the nurse. As my mother continued talking, I breathed a sigh of relief.

After the nurse's departure, we awaited the doctor. His presence was highly anticipated—every member of his office staff that we encountered had spoken so very highly of him. Eventually, he arrived. He was a small man, petite and fragile-looking. He glanced at my face and then launched directly into next steps. After he completed listing off his recommendations, he examined me briefly, keeping a careful distance between himself and the affected areas.

As his examination drew to a close, he offered a few concluding remarks and walked toward the door. Before he had time to usher us out, I hurriedly asked, "Will I ever be able to grow hair around my scars?"

"Why would that matter?" he said.

I asked again.

"Plastic surgery should provide all the correction necessary," he said.

Then he smiled and ran his hand through his hair. His eyes brightened as he went on to talk about previous patients and the operations he had conducted.

My parents and I continued to ask questions. Each time, the doctor responded before we had completed our sentences while flipping his hair. He stood at the other end of the room from where I sat on the examination table.

He continued talking about his other patients, saying that he had seen far worse than my case. In a flash of courage, I attempted to turn the tables.

"If you had a burn on your face, would it bother you?" I asked.

He shot a look of shock mixed with horror my way, before responding, "It wouldn't ever happen to me," he said, adding one last flip of his hair for good measure.

After that, Dr. Hair-Flip walked out of the room. We followed suit shortly after, traveling back through the corridors of the hospital.

RE-LEARNING TO SHAVE

The man who removes a mountain begins
by carrying away small stones.
—William Faulkner

Nearly two months after the accident, I was ready to shave.

My stubble had grown into long, wispy hairs in the weeks following the accident. While I welcomed the presence of facial hair as a way to obscure my scars, I struggled with certain aspects of my new appearance. For instance, I found the hair on my chin extremely bothersome. I was unable to grow hair in the center of my chin due to a scar, but the rest of the bristles encompassing the sides of my chin rubbed up against my scar, producing a sort of comb-over effect.

As a result, I made a habit of tugging at this tuft of hair throughout the day. So much so that as the day wore on, my face would hurt. To make matters worse, the absence of facial hair in the center of my chin added to my already sizeable insecurities regarding my appearance. Daunted at the idea of shaving for the first time after the accident, I resolved that doing so would be the best option. I couldn't remain bearded forever.

I took one last look in the mirror before lathering my face with shaving cream. I mentally traced the areas I needed to avoid, shaking at the thought of accidentally cutting my scars. After applying shaving cream, I placed the razor under the running water and brought the blade toward the right side of my face. I pulled the razor downwards in a single stroke, aided by the fact that this side of my face was free from scars. After each notch was removed, I rinsed my razor under warm water in the sink. I watched the hair fall off the razor, circling the drain before it disappeared.

My first challenge was my chin. I gingerly shaved around the tiny divot in my chin, pulling the razor away whenever I felt close to the scar. My upper lip was even harder to navigate with the large scar under my nose. A few extraneous, lightly colored hairs just above my lip proved too hard to reach. I left them as they were before putting my razor down on the edge of the sink triumphantly.

I took a good look in the mirror. The exposed scars, more evident now than before, jumped out at me. I shuddered upon seeing my clean-shaven face for the first time since the accident and immediately felt regret. I tried to soothe my rising sense of panic. *I can grow another beard*, I reminded myself, deciding I would do just that to conceal my scars.

When my mother saw my shaved faced for the first time, she looked shocked. "Your father is not going to be happy," she said.

Minutes later, he arrived. He walked into the living room to put down his bag and didn't notice my appearance right away. After putting various things away, he looked up, his face tinged with sadness. "You shaved," he said. He was upset. I felt like he didn't like seeing me cleanshaven, but I didn't know why. *Should I have waited to shave?* I wondered.

CUTTING WORDS

With friends like these, who needs enemies?
—Unknown

As my sixteenth birthday approached, I was hardly in a celebratory mood. Still on homebound tutoring, I rarely left the house. I was beginning to feel like a shut-in and longed for the opportunity to travel outside my home.

My hair was getting longer—it had been months since I had had a haircut. The hair around my ears was beginning to bother me, as was the hair coming down in the back, forming a tail approaching my neck. One night, when mom was out, my father took me to get a haircut. We purposefully waited until Saturday evening, hoping to find the shop mostly empty. Although my father never said so, I guessed that he wanted me to look nice on my birthday or to have some shred of normalcy during these tumultuous times.

I made an agreement with my father moments before we arrived at the barbershop. Neither of us would tell the barber about the accident.

There was no line when we arrived at the shop, and the barber asked me how I wanted my hair to look. Once receiving my specifications, he snipped and cut.

"What is that on your face?" he asked.

The hair on the back of my neck stood straight up, and I felt goosebumps on my arms. I had dreaded this moment. The question never got any easier to answer no matter how many times it was asked.

I blinked rapidly. I responded, telling the barber that I had been in an accident. He expressed surprise upon hearing my account. I quickly changed the subject, turning the conversation back to him. He acquiesced, pivoting toward more comfortable topics. I breathed a sigh of relief, not knowing that this exchange would become a pattern in many future conversations.

A few weeks later, when I returned to church for the first time, it became clear. My first night back fell on Bible Character Night, an activity intended to put a Christian spin on Halloween. Instead of dressing up as superheroes, kids dressed as their favorite Bible characters. High school students and volunteers were stationed throughout the church, distributing candy to all of the younger participants.

Expecting a hearty homecoming after the accident, I nervously readied myself to come into contact with literally hundreds of people. I was excited to return to the familiarity of my church home, and my expectations were high.

The lighting in the room was dim, helping to dull the impact of viewing my scarred face. I stood with a friend at a corner of a long hall in the church. Waves of children approached, eager to receive candy. A few children, when they saw me, grimaced at my face, and then ran away toward their parents. Others didn't seem to notice, more focused on the candy than my appearance. Some children asked a few innocent questions, although I avoided much explanation.

The children's responses were one thing—I was much more unsettled by the responses I received from adults. One woman, a friend who had watched my siblings and me grow up, came racing toward us.

"Was your brother the one who was in a horrible accident?" she asked me.

"No," I said. "That was me."

"Well, you look great!" she said. "It's a miracle you survived."

After a few more remarks, she ended our interaction by pointing at my face and confidently exclaiming, "There is nothing there!"

Future encounters mirrored this one. A few weeks later, I was back at church having a conversation with friends. I was filling them in on details of the accident when a couple walked up and started listening in. I was pointing out the scars on my face when the woman interrupted to say, "Don't worry, you will still find someone to marry you." She continued, "Don't worry, this isn't genetic, so your kids won't get it." I didn't know how to respond. "Well no," I wanted to say, "I am painfully aware of the fact that I was not born with these scars."

One of the most memorable encounters involved a longtime friend of my parents who was a respected member of our church community. Pulling me aside one night after a church event, he had a serious look on his face. He began to explain the spiritual forces at work pertaining to the accident.

"My family and I have prayed a lot about this," he said. "Our prayers have led us to believe that this was not your fault." He then explained that the accident had nothing to do with any sinful actions on my part.

"We believe it was due to the sinful actions committed by your parents," he said.

I laughed, thinking he was making a joke. After a few seconds, I realized his face had not moved and that he was serious.

SEIZING DEFEAT FROM THE JAWS OF VICTORY

No one is so brave that he is not disturbed
by something unexpected.
—Julius Caesar

A few weeks after the accident, I had a follow-up appointment with my plastic surgeon, Dr. Hair-Flip. I was experiencing a near-constant runny nose, and I asked if this was cause for concern. "No," he said quickly. After a brief examination, he said I was clear to return to school.

The nurse arranged for a professional-looking exemption waiver with the doctor's signature emblazoned at the top of the office's letterhead. I smiled at the thought of returning to school, to my old life.

Within days, my stuffiness and runny nose morphed into a cold. My cold progressively got worse and eventually turned into a full-blown sinus infection. Concerned by this development, my mother made an appointment for me with an ear, nose, and throat doctor (ENT).

Dr. Martin was balding, short, and stocky. He looked at my nose intently, surveying every inch.

"How did this happen?" he asked.

Once again, I looked to my mother, and she jumped in, explaining the circumstances surrounding my injuries.

After all of his questions had been answered, Dr. Martin brought a large, black contraption resembling a Darth Vader mask into the room. He carefully selected a part of the machine that looked like the tentacle of an octopus. Stringing a feeler through my right nostril, he provided detailed commentary while inspecting the inner workings of my nose. The second this object entered my nasal passage, my eyes began to water, increasing as the tentacle was pushed farther into my nose.

After careful examination, he retrieved the feeler and put away his tools before offering analysis. With a troubled look on his face, he informed us that upon impact, the acid made its way up my nostril. Along with several places on my face, neck, ears, and arms, the inside of my nose had been badly burned. Furthermore, the doctor found evidence of a developing staph infection in my nostril. This meant that I was susceptible to contracting a bacterial infection.

I attempted to process this news. *How were we just finding this out now?* I wondered.

The doctor said I should not return to school, instead recommending that I receive homebound instruction. As my mother and I talked in the car after the appointment, we decided to heed the doctor's advice—I would not return to school.

In the years to come, my sinuses would continue to flare up, usually at the most inopportune times—right before surgeries, school days, or other important events. Only after visiting another ENT years later did I learn the true extent of my injuries. The liquid acid had burned about an inch and a half up the inside of my nose, and the fumes had funneled through my entire respiratory system. The ENT said this put me at risk for frequent sinus infections and excess fluid buildup in my ears.

I did not, however, know all of that at the time. As we drove back home, I felt a stinging sense of defeat. My heart had been set on returning to school, as I was eager to return to normal. I worried about getting an infection, wondering how that would affect my recovery. The weather was downcast, and rain was falling precipitously. As I watched the raindrops fall onto the car windows, I tried to adjust to the idea of remaining at home for the foreseeable future.

A FATEFUL RETURN

Tragedy is like strong acid—it dissolves
away all but the very gold of truth.
—D.H. Lawrence

I spent most of the fall in homebound tutoring. This meant that unlike my peers, my school day began at 4 p.m. Each day, teachers arrived at my home and stayed well into the evening, providing instruction at my parents' dining room table.

At first, I struggled with this new schedule. I found it hard to focus on schoolwork. I was still adjusting to reading because the burns on my eyelids made it painful to keep my eyes open. Eventually, I established a routine and felt more comfortable with having school at home, although I felt lost and disconnected throughout, unsure of who I was after all that had happened. School seemed to pale in comparison to all that I was battling at the time.

After careful consideration by a team of doctors and teachers, we all agreed that I would return to regular school in early November, allowing plenty of time for preparations. I was overcome with a sense of nervousness as the date quickly approached. I worried about the reaction I would receive from my fellow classmates. I wondered how noticeable my scars would be to them and if I would experience any forms of bullying as a result of my change in appearance.

A few days before my return, I visited with faculty. I wanted the teachers to have an opportunity to get accustomed to my appearance in order to avoid any surprises or reactions that they might have in front of a classroom of students.

Our first stop was the guidance office. When my guidance counselor, Mr. Drake, saw me, his eyes brimmed with emotion. He embraced me in a giant hug. Before long, we were in tears, standing outside the hallway across from the empty cafeteria.

"Can I look?" he asked me gently.

I nodded my head. I watched his eyes trace each scar. He seemed surprised by what he saw, saying that he had expected the damage to be worse.

During our visit, Mr. Drake made it clear that I was not expected to make it through each full school day, especially during the first few weeks. If I needed to go home early, I could. However, I was determined to attend all of my classes each day. I wanted to be like every other student and to return to normalcy.

WHERE'S THAT ROOM?

I would far rather be ignorant than
wise in the foreboding of evil.
—Aeschylus

On my first day back at school in mid-November, I noticed a slight change to my class schedule. Mr. Drake had changed my study hall room. I didn't notice the alteration until I was unable to find the classroom as I navigated the school for the first time since the accident.

I trudged up the stairs, fighting my way through the crowded hallways. Students were everywhere, invading every corner of the school. As I put one foot in front of the other, I kept my face down, worrying that one of the students would accidentally hit my face. I ducked as someone inadvertently swung their backpack in my direction. It felt strange to be back. I felt lost in a place that had once been familiar. Most of the day passed by in a blur. I saw a few friends during the day—most were nice but standoffish, as if they didn't know how to interact with me now.

I finally reached the room I was looking for. The study hall monitor, a kind English teacher, greeted me. Despite her calming presence, I had a weird feeling about this last-minute change in my schedule. I brushed off the feelings, chalking them up to first-day jitters.

However, my sense of discomfort only increased with each week. I went on high alert whenever a specific man walked into the room. He was the teacher who taught in the room whenever the study hall wasn't occurring. He entered the space from time to time, looking disheveled, and glanced at me every so often. I tried to ignore his stares. After all, at this point, it didn't seem very unusual for someone to stare at me.

He entered at unexpected moments, shuffling items around the room or retrieving various papers. Sometimes he spent a few moments in the classroom, while other times he remained for more than half the period. Yet whenever he arrived, I felt uneasy. At the time, I knew nothing about this teacher—not even his name—but that would change soon enough.

PLUMBING THE DEPTHS

Facing it, always facing it, that's the
way to get through. Face it.
—Joseph Conrad

On my first day back at school, I made it through the first three blocks
of classes but was overcome with exhaustion as I approached my last
block of the day—physical education. Remembering Mr. Drake's urge
to find him if I felt overwhelmed, I made my way to the guidance office.
The next thing I knew, I had been whisked away to the front office.
Sitting in an uncomfortable chair near the door, I closed my eyes,
nearly falling asleep. My mind felt empty. It felt similar to waking up
after being under anesthesia.

Mr. Drake, upon seeing my closed eyes and sullen body language,
placed his hand on the arm of the chair and leaned down. With a
big smile on his face, he congratulated me on getting through most

of the day. My mother arrived soon after, and they both commented on the fact that I had made it through far more of the day than they expected. They seemed hopeful that in time I would readjust. After a few minutes of chatting, Mr. Drake asked, "Are you ready to go home?"

With each succeeding day, I fared a little better. I continued the practice of leaving school early or arriving to school late as I worked to become more acclimated. I tried to call upon Mr. Drake as little as possible as I was determined to rely upon my own strength. Yet a few weeks into my transition, I sat quietly in Mr. Drake's office attempting to make sense of the emotions swirling within me.

Mr. Drake sat in a big, black chair behind his desk, one hand covering his mouth. He raised his eyes every few seconds to meet my gaze, only to quickly drop them again and look away. The room was uncharacteristically silent. I longed to say something, to ask the questions burning holes in my mind. I wondered if my scars would always set me apart. I wondered how I would react if my appearance never changed. I felt alone and unlovable. I felt like something was deeply wrong with me, and I worried that my emotions had taken charge of me. Finally, I found the courage to ask the one question that had lodged inside me since the day everything changed.

"Why did this happen to me?" I asked Mr. Drake. "Tell me why this happened to me."

I let the question hang for a moment while I stared directly at him. He remained silent. I asked him if he had anything to say, any words to offer me as I tried to grab onto some sort of lifeboat to keep from drowning.

"There is no road map," he told me quietly.

Due to his busy schedule, Mr. Drake was not always available to meet. In the weeks after my return to school, he told me that Elaine Taylor, a new counselor, would sit in on our sessions and meet with me when he was unavailable. During those occurrences, she and I would meet in the conference room, sometimes as often as a few times a week.

One morning, I found myself in a particularly reflective mood. As I ruminated in the conference room, Ms. Taylor sat beside me wearing an off-white pantsuit. She didn't say much other than to inform me that she saw her primary role as that of being an active listener.

"There aren't many answers," she said.

This fit with the pattern of behavior she had exhibited in our lengthy sessions. She refrained from saying much, usually interjecting only to ask a question or to make a clarifying comment. She was quiet and thoughtful, often averting her eyes to avoid staring at my face for too long. She tried her best, but I got the feeling that she was slightly in over her head.

Our conversation that day centered around the idea of loss. I felt as if something had been robbed from me prematurely. I had trouble articulating this feeling, struggling to find the words to describe the emotions swirling within me. I told her I was having trouble focusing in my classes, unable to force the scene of the accident out of my head.

She listened carefully before asking a question of her own.

"Have you ever heard of the five stages of grief—denial, anger, bargaining, depression, and acceptance?"

Shortly before this, I had seen these five stages on display during an episode of the famed '90s sitcom, *Frasier*. Hours spent at home had introduced this show to me as I watched old episodes on television. In this particular episode, Frasier had lost his job, causing him to wrestle with these emotions as he tried to find a way to cope with the loss. Sometimes, he experienced all of the stages at once, vacillating between fits of anger and extreme sadness.

"Is it possible to experience more than one of these at the same time?" I asked.

"Yes, I think so," Ms. Taylor answered.

"I wonder how long it will take for me to reach a place of acceptance," I said a bit ruefully. I felt as if that particular milestone was so far away. In my head, I assumed that this stage would remain nearly impossible to fully access for months, if not years.

"It's a process," she told me. "Just take it one day at a time."

I tried to formulate how to live this out in my daily life. I asked if I should allow myself to feel the intensity of the feelings, despite how overwhelming they were sometimes. *What does healthy grieving look like?* I wondered.

"I think you'll have to find those answers out for yourself," Ms. Taylor said.

GROWING PAINS

In a world where you can be anything, be kind.
—Unknown

Upon my return to school, my schedule was not at all regular. Frequent doctor's appointments made my hours there rather unpredictable.

I was greeted each morning by the attendance secretary, Mrs. Kerry, a caring and compassionate woman who consistently made an effort to cheer me up each and every time I visited her cube. "How are you?" she would always ask. As we established a rapport, I eventually became a bit more open with her about my struggles, admitting how hard my daily life had become. One day, after asking how I was, she surprised me with her response. "Whenever I am feeling bad about my life, I watch the news to see that other people have it worse," she said. I couldn't recall ever watching the news as a child. Her words prompted me to wonder whether I should start.

One morning, after I checked in for the day, I was greeted by my science teacher from the previous year. "I have been looking for you," Mr. Harper said excitedly. As we caught up for a few moments, he referenced the accident and asked, "Was it a car accident?"

In response, I offered him the CliffsNotes version of my story. As he quietly listened, a look of knowing empathy crossed his face. Moments later, he asked me to accompany him back to his classroom, and I followed him down the hall.

Once we reached the classroom, he walked towards a large wooden cabinet near the edge of the room. "I have something for you," he said as he reached into the cabinet. When his hand reappeared, he was holding a pack of pads encased in white plastic with big, green letters emblazoned across the top.

CURAD. We Help Heal.
Scar Therapy Silicone Pads

The words jumped out at me causing my heart to race with excitement. *Could this help my scars?* I wondered.

"I was in a motorcycle accident," Mr. Harper said, detailing the extent of his scarring. His recovery included the use of these silicone pads, which helped restore his face to its former likeness. I had always known him to have a beard. I now wondered if this was grown in response to the accident he had endured.

"These pads work," he told me. "And I think they will work for you, too."

In the weeks that followed, I dutifully applied this newfound remedy each night before bed, placing the silicone pads directly over the affected areas. The pads fit best on the scars on my neck, especially the one that looked like a cat had dragged its claws through my skin. The other spots were trickier, especially the one underneath my jawline, which the pad failed to fully encompass.

Each night, I looked closely in the mirror, examining my face to see if the pads were working. I wanted to see that the redness was receding, that the scars were shrinking, but I never detected any noticeable improvements in their appearance. After applying the pads consistently for a time, I stopped, turning to other remedies that would hopefully produce better results.

Over the years, I employed a long litany of methods—pills and pads, ointments and lotions, cleaning solutions and vitamin mixes, surgeries and lasers, soaps and diets, along with countless other treatments. My parents were faithful in providing a myriad of remedies, suggesting new products on a regular basis. Each yielded few results, but at the time, when Mr. Harper first gave me the scar therapy pads, all I could feel was a burst of hope.

Mr. Harper and I parted ways soon after. He asked me to keep him posted on my progress and wished me well. I never saw him again, yet even now, I still have that very first pad. It reminds me of one man's kindness and the tangible symbol of hope that he graciously offered to me at a time when I needed it most.

HIDE AND SEEK

Vanity is the quicksand of reason.
—George Sand

After two appointments with the hair-flipping plastic surgeon, my parents and I determined it was time to leave Children's Hospital behind. Based on the referral of a friend, my mother made an appointment with a doctor at a practice in Georgetown.

Upon our arrival, I immediately noticed the top-of-the-line artwork on display, accompanied by the dozens of awards and numerous degrees scattered along the walls. The shiny office in downtown Washington reeked of importance; and, it was clear by the impressive looking furniture and decorations adorning the room that the practice was quite successful.

My mother and I sat in the lobby. Suddenly, my eyes were drawn to a man behind the door on the other side of the room dressed in slacks and a button-down shirt. He appeared to work there, although his position within the practice was unclear. During our nearly one-hour wait, he repeatedly popped his head out of a back office and into the waiting room. Then he would disappear, only to reappear moments later, waving in our direction.

Eventually, we were led to a patient room. After several more minutes of waiting, in walked the staff member I had spotted while in the lobby. Turns out he was the doctor. *How did he have time to repeatedly check on the waiting room while his patients piled up waiting to see him?* I wondered.

Dr. Randall was a thin, quiet man with hair speckled gray. His teeth were perfectly white. He had a five-o'clock shadow and almost perfect posture. He spoke confidently and quickly, leaving very little room for interpretation.

Despite his confidence, Dr. Randall's handshake was weak. In time, he told me that his constant stubble was actually the result of a laser procedure that stopped the growth of his facial hair. He would never have to shave again. He exclaimed proudly that he "saved a lot of time each morning." No wonder he had time to peer at his patients while they sat in his waiting room.

This scene played out over the next several appointments. Dr. Randall paced back and forth from one end of his office to the other. He would stop at the doorway, standing still for a few moments, staring ahead—as if he had completely forgotten where he was or what he was doing. After a few seconds, he would walk back into the office and disappear once again, only to reappear moments later to wave at his patients.

Dr. Randall was a man of few words. During our first appointment, he asked about the circumstances surrounding my accident. As my mother shared what happened, I watched Dr. Randall. His face remained unchanged as he absorbed my mother's words.

In our first visit, he suggested a round of steroid injections. The desired outcome, as I understood it, was to flatten the surface of the affected areas, as well as reduce the redness of the scars. To lessen the pain, Dr. Randall would inject lidocaine into the areas that would be treated. The lidocaine, acting as an anesthetic, was intended to numb the area.

After waiting a few minutes for the lidocaine to set in, the doctor approached me brandishing a long needle. The moment the needle met my skin, searing pain shot through my body. He injected the skin under my nose and at the top of my forehead. He was effectively boring little holes into my skin in an effort to break up the scar tissue. It felt as if someone was taking a knife and carving my face, making me want to scream out in pain.

The nights that followed these gut-wrenching sessions were filled with torturous dreams. There was one recurring dream, a particularly upsetting one. It began in an alley where I was walking carefully, minding my own business. The alley was empty with no one in sight. Suddenly, out of nowhere, a stranger appeared. Then another. And another. And another. Approaching me cautiously, they uttered no words. Terrified, my body stiffened, trying to make sense of my surroundings. What did I have that they wanted? What did I do wrong?

Suddenly, one of them reached into his pocket and produced a knife large enough to induce fear. Brandishing it, he lunged at me, cutting deep into my skin. Following this misguided fellow's example, the others followed suit, making mincemeat of my face.

"NO!" I screamed, begging them to stop.

Oblivious to my cries, the men kept cutting, carving up my face one gash at a time. Just as I was beginning to wonder whether I would live through the attack, I would wake up, overcome with fear and shocked by the intensity of the sensations I experienced during the dream.

After a few more rounds of injections, Dr. Randall realized that more intervention would be necessary in order to reduce both the size and the appearance of the scars. The steroids were doing little to flatten the appearance of the scars, or to reduce the redness. My nose remained in danger of collapsing, especially my right nostril.

As a result, he recommended a surgical operation. He offered few details other than to say something about taking skin from behind my right ear and placing it under my nose—acting as a sort of skin graft. It all sounded simple enough with the consequences nearly null.

"What about the incision behind my ear?" I asked. "Will it be noticeable?"

"It will be so small not even your barber will notice it," he said. With that, I agreed to undergo surgery at the doctor's direction.

A few weeks later at our next appointment, the doctor was unable to join us. As a result, he sent one of his nurses, Joy, in his stead. This was to be our last appointment before the scheduled upcoming surgery. Joy was a slender woman with long, stylish black hair. Her face was covered with a heavy layer of makeup, along with mascara heavily applied around her eyes.

She began the appointment by producing a legal waiver for which a signature was required in advance of the impending surgery. Reading through the legal clauses, I readily understood that I would be releasing Dr. Randall and his practice from any and all liability if complications or fatalities occurred as a result of this medical procedure. The risks were laid out quite plainly, including possible blindness or death as a result of the effects of anesthesia. Considering that I had been exposed to such dangers in the not-so-distant past, I bristled as my eyes caught sight of those two complications in particular. As Joy steered the conversation towards covering the extreme risks, she emphasized that these risks were "unlikely to occur." In spite of her assurances, I continued feeling overwhelmed by a sense of foreboding. Hadn't the last few months proved that I was no stranger to experiencing unlikely circumstances?

Despite my misgivings, I remained mostly quiet. I assumed that the look of horror likely encompassing my face would be enough to alert the nurse to my growing levels of discomfort. As the appointment continued, it became clear that my facial expressions were not enough to communicate my inner feelings. She passed the time by engaging in small talk and avoided offering any details pertaining to my upcoming surgery.

Finally, I decided to ask questions.

"What will I look like after the surgery?" I asked.

"I don't know," she responded. "You'll have to ask Dr. Randall."

My father posed additional queries, but the nurse redirected us once again to speak with the doctor despite the fact that he was not in the room.

"What should I do to prepare for surgery?" I asked.

"Don't change anything with your exercise routine," she said. "You never know with anesthesia."

Her words caught me off guard. I wasn't quite sure what she meant. What about anesthesia made it more dangerous than any other part of the operation? Worried, I began to question whether or not to go forward with the operation. It all seemed too dangerous, the risks too high and the opportunity for failure quite possible and severe. Even if these risks were unlikely to materialize, were any of these complications more far-fetched than getting burned with sulfuric acid?

Since asking questions appeared futile, we stopped and allowed the nurse to guide the conversation. She talked about past patients, her home life, and her exercise routine, smiling from ear to ear as she conducted the conversation mostly with herself.

Sitting on the examination table, my mind began to race. Dr. Randall had broached the subject of surgery rather nonchalantly just a few weeks before, making it sound like an easy procedure with very little risk. *Bring him back in here,* I wanted to say. *This isn't what I signed up for.*

UNEARTHING THE PAST

Though he slay me, I will hope in him; yet
I will argue my ways to his face.
—Job 13:15

One night I laid awake in bed, staring up at the ceiling. I couldn't fall asleep. I was thinking about how hard everything felt—how hard school was, how hard it was to get through the day. I felt abandoned by many of my friends. I was desperately unhappy and in a lot of pain. I felt like no woman would ever look at me, see my face, and fall in love with me. I thought about how hard this continued to be, each and every day. Pulling myself out of bed each morning had become a chore. Showering was difficult, both physically and emotionally. I hadn't been able to exercise since the accident. I couldn't even be in the sunlight without worrying about my scars. I spent hours in hospital rooms, doctor's offices, and waiting rooms. It was months after the accident, and at every turn I heard about the need for more surgeries and medical treatments. That night, I wished I had died in the accident. It would have been easier.

So many people were telling me how miraculous it was that I had survived the accident. I should have died. At the very least I should have lost my eyesight. Instead, I scraped by—and it was a miracle— but it felt like a half shell of the life I had once lived. Death seemed like the only way out.

I felt ashamed even entertaining such thoughts. Yet they continued unabated. Throughout the day I was usually able to keep my mind away from suicidal ideations, but at night it was harder to control my tired mind. I continued to wonder whether my life had become too arduous to keep on living. Occasionally, I combatted such dangerous thoughts by pacing around the lower levels of the house late at night to avoid waking up the rest of the family.

On such nights, I typically sought out the last picture of me from before the accident. It had been taken in May of 2009 and was on display in the living room. It was an image of me wearing an oversized Washington Capitals T-shirt, smiling widely as I accepted an award on stage at my church. During these clandestine viewing sessions, I nearly always pulled the brown frame down from the bookshelf on which it was resting, using my hand to trace the outline of my previous face along the glass.

It was also during these tense moments that I decided that suicide was not an option. It would be far too painful for my family. My life had nearly ended once already—I could not end it only a few months into my recovery. My love for the four members of my family kept me alive. I believed they were worth living for, even if I was not.

A CHANGE IN COURSE

The doctor should be opaque to his patients and, like a mirror,
should show them nothing but what is shown to him.
—Sigmund Freud

Three months after the accident, I finally agreed to see a psychiatrist. I had been determined to conquer my mental health struggles on my own, but my recent suicidal thoughts led me to consider seeking professional help.

When I arrived at the psychiatrist's office, my eyes were drawn to a large bookcase along the wall. The shelves were filled with medical journals and works of literature. A sofa sat in the middle of the room, piled with decorative pillows. A tissue box rested on a simple nightstand.

My appointment was with a man named Dr. Leo. He was a balding, middle-aged, white man with brown hair on both sides of his head.

He was thin with a runner's build and wore a button-down shirt with dress pants. He was tall and serious-looking, with an imposing presence. He chose his words carefully and spoke with a measure of authority.

Dr. Leo came into the room and started asking me questions, inquiring as to the reason for my visit. As the consultation unfolded, he rubbed his chin, looking intrigued. He sat in a large, black chair directly across from his desk, and peered at me through his brown glasses.

Dr. Leo asked many questions about my symptoms. I described my anger and irritability. I spoke of my low energy and how difficult it was for me to get out of bed each morning. I described how lethargic and exhausted I felt and how hard it was for me to control my emotions or to focus on much else outside the loss of my face.

These symptoms seemed to pique his curiosity. Instead of standing up, he wheeled himself over to the bookshelf on the opposite wall, his black chair gliding seamlessly along the dark carpet. He reached for a large book labeled *Diagnostic and Statistical Manual of Mental Disorders* on the spine. His finger skimmed the table of contents and then he carefully flipped to a page.

He scanned the page, mumbling some of the symptoms I had discussed. Finally, he swiveled around.

"I believe you exhibit symptoms of post-traumatic stress disorder," he said with a wry smile, revealing understated excitement.

This diagnosis surprised me. In the months since the accident I had never once thought that I was experiencing symptoms of PTSD. Depression seemed far more likely. After all, wasn't PTSD a condition reserved for soldiers returning from battle?

"It is quite common in patients who have experienced trauma," Dr. Leo said.

After revealing the diagnosis, Dr. Leo turned the conversation toward faith. He asked what religion I identified with.

I told him that I considered myself to be a non-denominational Christian. Dr. Leo asked if he could incorporate faith into future sessions, and I agreed. He smiled.

Soon after, the appointment came to a close. *The doctor seems nice enough,* I thought. Board certified in general psychiatry and child and adolescent psychiatry, Dr. Leo appeared to be more than qualified to take on my case.

On our way out, the sun peeked into the room, coming through the window behind the same couch I had occupied for the last hour. The view was of the forest, its trees without leaves in the middle of winter. Despite the cold and bleak outlook, the sun shone brightly. The scene mirrored the newfound hope I felt that Dr. Leo could help bring a change in season to my own life, helping me to transition my emotional winter into a beautiful spring.

Over the course of my first several sessions with Dr. Leo, we discussed different treatment options at length. Before considering prescribing medication, he suggested an alternative treatment that might help mitigate the PTSD symptoms I was experiencing: irritability, re-living the accident, persistent insomnia, flashbacks, and nightmares. Dr. Leo recommended a therapist specializing in Eye Movement Desensitization and Reprocessing (EMDR) treatment. He mentioned something about this course of treatment possibly decreasing the level of irritability I experienced. He also thought it might soften my outlook on life while allowing me to catch a few additional hours of sleep at night instead of spending countless hours lying awake.

Upon meeting Mr. Evans, he immediately struck me as a kindly fellow. He possessed a jovial sense of humor, which often caused him to break out into a wide smile or a hearty laugh. A balding, overweight man with a mustache, he made me feel safe from the very beginning, carefully explaining the mechanics of EMDR therapy.

As a licensed professional counselor (LPC), he was qualified to administer this form of treatment. He explained that EMDR was a short-term treatment, intended to help lessen the intensity of the emotions experienced as a result of a traumatic event. The key was to revisit that scene and help unpack the complicated feelings in order to facilitate emotional healing.

The treatment would begin by him raising his finger and asking me to follow his finger with my eyes. He would wave his finger back and forth, first to the left and then to the right. My eyes followed his finger, remaining trained on his every move. An odd feeling overcame me, evoked by a sense that this exercise was all too similar to hypnosis. His finger led me into the past, some episodes from years before.

Round and round we went, different images appearing in my mind's eye. My childhood home. The hill where my life changed forever. My family members. My body writhing in pain. It felt a bit like watching a rerun of a television show as I viewed past episodes of my life. After a while, Mr. Evans would stop moving his finger and subsequently ask me to describe the scene in detail. We would analyze the meaning behind the event and then his finger would rise again, leading me to another destination in my past.

Some of the details of the accident that I had previously blocked from my memory came flooding back during these sessions. I started to remember even the tiniest of details, down to the smells and sounds of that fateful day. I re-lived that moment—when I tossed the box onto the cement slab as I was told—and the explosion that followed. The ringing in my ears was so loud, as if I was experiencing the event all over again in the present.

At the end of our sessions, Mr. Evans would leave time to further analyze how the sequence of events fit together. The conversation would reveal unpredictable patterns, helping me to come to terms with the trauma I experienced. Having the ability to confront the accident head-on from the safety of a doctor's office began to help the aftereffects wash away. Little by little, I was able to make sense of the past by placing a healthy distance between myself and the event. This distance allowed me to unpack emotions and helped mitigate some of the emotional side effects of the accident, such as flashbacks. Going forward, instead of re-living the accident, I could view that day as if from a television. Reasoning through any emotions that arose as a result of a flashback helped me develop the strength to be able to turn off the screen instead of remaining a hostage inside my own brain.

After a few months of sessions, Mr. Evans told me that he believed that I had accomplished all I could through EMDR therapy. The next step, he said, was for me to return to regularly meeting with Dr. Leo. He offered words of encouragement by sharing bits of his own journey, suggesting that a rich life could indeed be found even after tragedy. He wished me well and sent me off to continue conquering the demons from my past, one day at a time.

FEARING THE WORST

Who looks outside, dreams; who looks inside, awakes.
Carl Jung

After undergoing EMDR treatment, I re-commenced regular sessions with Dr. Leo. After hearing me describe my symptoms over the course of a few sessions, he asked, "Have you considered medication?" At first, I dismissed the suggestion. I wanted to conquer this on my own—I didn't need the assistance of prescription medication, I reasoned.

He seemed surprised by my reticence, since in our initial sessions I had agreed to a prescription for Ambien and then Ativan, both intended to assist me in falling asleep. Yet those were short-term medications intended to be taken only a for a limited duration. I was nervous at the thought of filling a prescription intended for a longer-term period to manage symptoms that felt far less pressing than being unable to sleep.

In future sessions, Dr. Leo found a different way to talk about the possibility of adding medication as a part of my treatment. His urgency about medication grew with each passing week. However, I continued to resist.

"It's like having an illness and not taking an antibiotic," he said.

"Can't I do this on my own without medication?" I asked. Taking medication felt like admitting defeat.

"You are doing great work," he said. "But this traumatic event could have altered your hormone levels in a way that can only be corrected with medication. Medication is simply another tool in the toolbox."

He had described the therapeutic toolbox before as a chest filled with resources that could assist in my fight to ward off symptoms of PTSD and depression. Our sessions were part of this box, along with other techniques such as taking deep breaths during stressful situations. I learned to employ these strategies in my toolbox when I faced dark feelings.

"Go back to the toolbox," Dr. Leo said, "and if there isn't anything you can use, then medicine is a viable option."

His persistence paid off. I eventually decided to try medication. When I talked with my parents about taking medication for my PTSD and depressive symptoms, my father resisted.

"You can't go on medication," he said. "You will never be able to get a security clearance."

My father went on talking about the perils of medication. He declared that it would have serious future consequences. I understood my father's opposition, but I felt discouraged.

Several weeks later, I attended church with my family on Super Bowl Sunday. I was in good spirits, anticipating the football game later that evening and maintaining my pleasant mood for the duration of the service.

That is, until the sermon concluded. I suddenly felt on edge. My mind began to race, and dizziness overcame me. I felt disoriented and confused.

My family and I moved into the lobby while my anxiety mounted. I could feel my heart rate quickening, and my hands began to shake slightly. I tried to quell my feelings by taking deep breaths and utilizing logic to calm myself down.

It didn't work. After a few minutes, I decided to wait for my family in the car. I turned toward my father and asked him for the keys to the car. He looked surprised, but walked with me to the car without asking questions. Climbing into the backseat, I felt relieved to be out of public view. After a few minutes, I regained my composure.

"What happened in there?" my father asked, after it was clear that I had calmed down.

I tried to explain. As I described my experience, he looked out the car window with his hand under his chin in contemplation.

"Sounds like you had a panic attack," he said.

The discussion veered toward medication. Seemingly moved by this episode, my father relaxed his previous position regarding medication, recognizing that it could help me heal. We sat quietly in the car contemplating next steps.

My mother appeared a little while after, opening the car door with a look of concern.

"What happened?" she said.

"He had a problem," my father said quietly. "I had to take him out." With that, we drove home knowing that something would have to change.

UNEXPECTED CONSEQUENCES

No action is without its side effects.
—Barry Commoner

At my next appointment with Dr. Leo, I told him about my panic attack and finally agreed to consider medication. He reviewed the pros and cons of an array of medications with me, then listed the possible side effects as if reading from a script. He mentioned dry mouth, nausea, insomnia. Some could even lead to an increase in suicidal thoughts. It all depended on body chemistry, physical makeup, and even state of mind. Most of the side effects sounded pretty standard. Except for one.

"It could cause you to have an erection lasting longer than four hours," the doctor said matter-of-factly. "If that happened, you would just go to the hospital."

I wasn't sure I heard him correctly. Four hours?

"It's painful," he said, but the hospital "would straighten everything out. Besides, this reaction occurs in fewer than one percent of patients," he said reassuringly.

I pondered his statement, trying to decide whether the one-percent risk was low enough to take the plunge.

"Wasn't the accident something that only happens to less than one percent of people?" I asked.

Dr. Leo turned away, quickly jotting a few words on his prescription pad. Apparently my statement swayed him toward prescribing a medication for me that did not pose this unpleasant side-effect. I felt as if I had dodged a bullet—or perhaps, more accurately, a long-lasting erection.

At first, medication proved to be an effective antidote. My ability to focus improved. My capacity to reason through situations increased. My anxiety abated. I felt more in control of my life, more empowered. Life felt easier to navigate.

As time went on, I did notice some side effects. While I was relieved that the intensity of my emotions had been dulled, I felt like the medication had a numbing effect. Instead of just tamping down my emotions, I felt like the medication had eradicated all of them. I also experienced bouts of dizziness and dry mouth, which I brought up with Dr. Leo at one of our subsequent sessions.

"Give it some time," Dr. Leo said. He advised me to stay the course while reminding me that it might take a few months for my body to adjust

In the process, I began to identify ways in which I could conquer my symptoms of PTSD and depression outside of medication. Looking back at the metaphorical toolbox I had assembled with the help of Dr. Leo, I identified the tools I could use to assuage the tide of depression that I could experience again if I chose to stop refilling my prescription.

After a few months, I told Dr. Leo I was ready to stop medication. This course of treatment had been very valuable, helping me to take the edge off of the emotional pain I was grappling with so that I could reason through how the past was affecting my present. I had a newfound sense of confidence, convinced that I had the tools to face whatever came next. I asked for his opinion, eager for him to validate my decision.

"It's up to you," he said with a smile. "It always has been."

GETTING AWAY

Maybe life isn't about avoiding the bruises. Maybe it's
about collecting the scars to prove we showed up for it.
—Unknown

The first time I drove a car by myself was one of the most exhilarating moments of my life.

It was March 2010 as I backed my mother's Honda out of the garage for the first time. I adjusted the mirror several times, ensuring that I would be able to see traffic from all angles once I made it onto the road. Pressing gently on the accelerator, I cautiously backed the car out of the driveway and into the street. Shifting gears from reverse into drive, I got a taste of sweet independence as I put my foot back on the gas pedal, feeling fully in control as I made my way to school.

I had received my license just days earlier, right before my parents departed on a trip to Florida. This was their first trip since the accident, and, although they didn't say it, I felt like they were a bit worried about leaving me alone.

In their absence, I stayed at a friend's house. On the first night, I sat on a couch with my friend and his mother, Evelyn. I began asking questions, knowing that Evelyn had been through a traumatic experience, too. I had heard the story before but wanted to hear more about her recovery.

Evelyn told me about being a teenager and driving with her best friend. Evelyn was driving when they were hit by a truck. Her best friend didn't survive the crash. Evelyn looked pained as she spoke, averting her eyes and looking down at her clasped knees.

Then Evelyn leaned forward as if to signal that she was about to impart something vital. I wondered if she had some wisdom about trauma based on her life experience. Since it had been decades since her own accident had occurred, I wondered if she had a richer perspective, enabling her to discover truths I still had yet to learn.

"So, what was it like?" I asked before faltering a bit. I looked down at my lap, struggling to summon the courage to probe deeper. Lifting my head, I looked into Evelyn's eyes. The pain in her eyes was palpable, as if the accident had just happened the day before. *Maybe I should stop*, I thought. It felt unfair to force someone to relive the past.

"No, no, it's okay," she said calmly. "It's important for you to understand."

Feeling emboldened after receiving her permission, I plowed ahead. "What . . ."

Just then, I heard my phone ring. She stood up to leave as I fished my phone out of my jeans.

"Go ahead. Take it," she said. "We will talk later."

As I put the phone to my ear, I could not help but hope that Evelyn and I could pick up where we left off. Sadly, we never returned to that conversation, and I've always wondered what could have been revealed if the moment had not been lost.

A few days later, I spent the last night of my parents' trip with family friends that I lovingly referred to as "Bubbe" and "Zayde," the words for grandmother and grandfather in Yiddish. Zayde was Jewish, and his family had escaped Germany before the Holocaust. Zayde met Bubbe years later, well after he had arrived in the United States. The couple was one of my favorites: they were full of good humor, wonderful storytellers, and gracious hosts.

After a lovely dinner and extended conversation that went on well into the night, it was time for bed. I retreated to the basement apartment, finding my way down the stairs and stopping at the foot of a large bed with white sheets in an adjacent room. As it was Friday night, I expected to be tired after what had been both an exciting and exhausting week. Yet no matter how hard I tried, I could not fall asleep. An example of my insomnia kicking in, likely aided by this new, unfamiliar sleep environment.

I repeatedly closed my eyes, attempting to force myself to sleep. After a few minutes, I caught sight of a small, portable television resting on a nearby desk. I climbed out of bed and turned on the television, thinking the background noise might lull me to sleep. A VHS tape sat atop the television: *As Good As It Gets*, a film starring Jack Nicholson. I had not previously seen this movie, but I figured that anything with Jack Nicholson was worth seeing at least once.

I was struck by one particular scene where Jack Nicholson's character barges into his psychiatrist's office. "You said you could help me!" he says in an exasperated tone. He rages at the psychiatrist before stomping out into the waiting room. Looking at the patients, he asks the group, "What if this is as good as it gets?"

In my next session with Dr. Leo, I posed the same question. I was really asking a multitude of questions wrapped in one. What if life would always be this way? What if my scars would always matter, the emotional and physical pain associated with them failing to lessen with the passage of time? What if I always felt and looked this way? What if the cure I was seeking did not exist, or possibly, existed for others but just not for me?

"I don't see why it has to be that way," Dr. Leo said. "What do you have that the character in the movie doesn't?"

"Youth?" I said. "*Not* a severe case of obsessive-compulsive disorder?"

"You have Jesus," Dr. Leo said.

Lord have mercy.

Maybe our sessions were as good as they were going to get.

TRAVELING IN CIRCLES ON AN EMPTY STOMACH

*True strength is holding it together when everyone
else would understand if you fell apart.*
—Unknown

Seven months after sulfuric acid had scarred my face, I found myself
preparing for my first major scar revision surgery. After changing
into the hospital gown provided by the nurses, I sat in a hospital bed
located within a large, spacious room. Nurses milled about asking
incessant questions. "Have you eaten this morning?" "No," I responded.
I wish, I thought to myself. "When was the last time you had a drink
of water?" a nurse asked. "Last night," I said, her words causing my
thirst to be brought to the forefront of my mind.

A few minutes later, she asked again, "When was the last time you
had a drink of water?"

"Last night," I answered again, feeling a bit of déjà vu.

I talked to the nurses, doing my best to distract myself from what was to come. The mild banter did much to ease the tension from the room. *It's okay to be scared*, they seemed to be saying. *Just keep listening to the sound of my voice. Everything was going to be fine.*

Eventually, a nurse approached me with a needle in her hand. She assured me that she would do her best not to hurt me. I warned her that my veins were notorious for rolling, deceiving the eyes of medical staff by disappearing moments after they have inserted the needle into my arm.

Pain enveloped me the moment the nurse stuck the needle into my arm. I could feel each prick as she moved the needle this way and that, causing a burst of pain to shoot up my arm with each movement. My arm became slightly bruised after my veins repeatedly disappeared. Eventually, she determined it might be better to try my left arm.

As the ordeal dragged on, I became agitated. The turn of events played into my already highly-charged emotions. The nurse, sensing my irritation, summoned a colleague, who approached me with a smile on her face. She looked at me softly, her gaze revealing kindness in her eyes. She talked softly and quietly.

Her calming presence lifted my spirits, especially after she successfully captured my vein, quickly taming its rolling ways. Maybe she was a vein whisperer, or her confidence was enough to finish the job. Grateful, my blood pressure began to return to normal levels. Soon after, my mother approached. Putting her hand on my hair, she patted my head softly, whispering in reassuring tones that everything was going to be okay.

For a moment, I believed her and felt strong enough to face whatever the future held. As the nurses wheeled me down to the operating room, a feeling of impending doom soon encircled me. My stomach was in knots, my chest felt heavier with each passing breath. *What if things go wrong?* I wondered. *What if I die on the table?*

"I love you," my mother said, telling me that she would be there when I woke up.

"I love you, too," I said.

With that, I was off, the nurses pushing me briskly through the corridors of the surgery center. The operating room was dark, making the figures milling about hard to accurately make out. Big silver bowls sat idly nearby, and a large fan was in the middle of the room whizzing at high speed. After a few moments, my awareness dimmed as images and incoming stimuli became increasingly fuzzy. My eyes floated aimlessly around the room as I strained to catch a glimpse of Dr. Randall. Suddenly, he was by my side, his hair concealed by a scrub cap.

"Is it going to be okay?" I asked. I felt as if he held the future of my scarred face, and my life, in his hands.

"I know it's going to be okay," he said. His face was filled with determination, his eyes betraying no trace of fear or uncertainty.

I hoped the confidence in his eyes could make its way into my own. I strained to keep my eyes open, replaying scenes from the eventful day in my head. Despite my misgivings, I resolved to stand firm. I hoped he knew what he was doing, because I sure didn't.

A NEW FACE

Wherever you go, there you are.
—Confucius

Washington, D.C. That wonderful, beautiful city recognized by people all around the world. A bustling town brimming with excitement, filled with people milling about, determined to reach their intended destinations as quickly as possible. Washington is unique, a place teeming with importance, where the man or woman standing next to you could be an adviser to the President. Normally I would revel in visiting this city, breathing in the Washington air as if it were the very last breath I would take on this earth.

This day, exactly one week after my first major scar revision surgery, was different.

I longed to hide my face from those passing by, avoiding their blank stares or looks of horror. I darted inside the door as fast as I could, eager to travel up the elevator to Dr. Randall's office. This was the day I had longed for all week—the removal of the cloths left behind after surgery. I was hopeful that once the doctor's handiwork was revealed, I would look whole again.

As I sat on the examination table, Dr. Randall began to extricate the cloths from my face. As his efforts got underway, it felt like he was ripping off layers of my skin piece by piece. With each snip of the stitches, pain shot up my nose and forehead. Memories came flooding back with roaring intensity, bringing me back to the initial days after the accident. *Please make it stop,* I thought to myself.

After he had completed his work, he handed me a mirror to inspect my new face. My eyes were immediately drawn to the outline of the freshly formed scars. My upper lip, the area in which my mustache was intended to grow, was crushed inward, as if someone had scooped out a large piece of skin and left a gaping hole in its wake. Shaken by this unexpected change in my appearance, I remained quiet, opting to say nothing in response to what I saw in the mirror. Everything slowed down, and it felt as if I was in a daze.

"It will look better in time," the doctor said.

Perhaps he was right, I thought to myself. After all, time has a way of healing even the most stubborn wounds.

After the appointment ended and my mother and I returned to the car, I pulled down the visor above the passenger seat, eager to take in another long look at my face. I barely recognized myself, as my upper lip appeared to be distorted. I was completely and utterly shocked by this outcome. I had been convinced that it would look far better than it did. "It looks like you have a cleft palate," my mother said.

During the car ride home, a feeling of strong disappointment filled my spirit. How could my face look worse than it had just a week before? This turn of events made me feel as if the pain and struggle of the past week were invalidated, leading me towards the conclusion that the whole ordeal had been a waste.

"I can't go back to school like this," I told my mother, sapped of energy. The surgery had been timed to correspond with my spring break, so I wouldn't have to miss additional school days. After spending spring break of my sophomore year holed up in my bedroom, I had hoped to return the following Monday along with my fellow classmates.

"I know," she said quietly.

We began discussing how much time off would be needed. In my deflated state, we decided on a week; it was enough time for me to heal before traveling back into the unknown. Relieved at hearing that I wouldn't be going back to school anytime soon, a wave of relaxation came over me. I sat back in my seat to ponder the doctor's words. Unsure of whether or not time would provide the ultimate cure, I tried my best to internalize the doctor's message, albeit halfheartedly. Even though it felt as if I would never be rid of the scars I so desperately wanted to eradicate.

HOPE IN A NEW DIRECTION

That best portion of a good man's life, His little nameless,
unremembered acts of kindness and of love.
—William Wordsworth, "Lines Composed a Few Miles above
Tintern Abbey"

The phone rang. Zayde was calling.

He was one of the faithful few who continually checked in, making an effort to call if he couldn't visit in person. Even in retirement, he was extremely busy, living an active lifestyle and giving back to his community, yet no matter how busy he got, he always made time for me.

I knew even then that his influence had made an indelible mark upon my life, his words and actions actively helping to shape both my perspective and character. Only after he suffered a heart attack when I was twelve did I come to realize how much he meant to me. He was my true grandfather, in every sense of the word.

He was calling to find out the results of my surgery. With most others, I would have hedged, carefully curating my response to exude positivity. Our relationship, however, had always been marked by a commitment to transparency. This interaction was no different. We spoke for a few minutes, during which my feelings readily emerged. In response, he suggested we meet for lunch, promising to pick me up so that we could go out and talk more. I hesitated, but my desire to avoid being seen in public gave way to a sense of love for this great man. I acquiesced.

A few hours later, he arrived. The moment of truth. *What would his reaction be? Would he look at me differently?* I wondered. I answered the door, bracing myself for the possibilities of the encounter.

True to his character, he didn't bat an eyelash upon seeing me, nor did he blink. He hugged me just as he always did, his warm embrace imbuing a sense of hope into my tired soul. We spoke for a few moments, his demeanor and body language mirroring all previous interactions. For a few moments, it felt as if he understood, or at least was trying to see the complete picture of all that had happened to me over the last week.

As we drove along the streets near my home, the conversation ebbed and flowed with a few moments of silence sprinkled in between. The man in the driver's seat sat tall, even though in reality he was quite short. A portly gentleman, his hair was streaked white, which gave away his advanced age. Yet his piercing eyes revealed someone far younger than he seemed: a man appearing to be somewhere in his mid-fifties, when in reality he was in his seventies. He carried a surprisingly strong sense of hope and an idealistic streak that drew me to him. He was full of youthful vigor and excitement for the future. He was the man I hoped to be someday.

Our conversation was nothing out of the ordinary. We talked about life and politics, philosophy and religion. It was reminiscent of the

Samuel Moore-Sobel

conversations we had always shared together. Even though my facial appearance had changed, Zayde's demeanor and topics of conversation never did. His enjoyment of my company did not waver even though my life had changed forever.

Over lunch, I shared with Zayde that I was seeking a job as a counselor of children with special needs at a nearby summer camp. "That's exactly what you should be doing!" he exclaimed happily, displaying that big hearty smile that seemed to envelop whoever was nearby. "That is exactly what you need. Being around kids, there is nothing like it." I knew he would be pleased, as he had consistently been encouraging me to look outside myself in the months since the accident. Having Zayde's blessing over my future plans meant the world to me. How could I not long for the approval of this man whom I greatly respected?

As I sat in the restaurant on that sunny April day looking as if I had a cleft palate, Zayde was the same as he always was. The bond we shared had always been special, which was why I had adopted him into our family long ago as my unofficial grandfather. For a moment, I forgot. I forgot what I looked like and instead chose to focus on him.

Sometimes nothing out of the ordinary has to happen for something to be remarkable.

WHO AM I?

Knowing yourself is the beginning of all wisdom.
—Aristotle

The bell rang. It was a hot day in June on the last day of school. They called it the bell, although it sounded more like a siren or a loud bellowing noise coming from deep within the center of the building. Masses of students were rushing past me. This was the part of the school day that I hated the most. I experienced a surge in adrenaline whenever I found myself traveling among students crowding the hallways. No matter how hard I tried to remain calm during school dismissal, I needed to find some peace and quiet during the height of the rush.

I ducked into the school library. At this time of the day, it was almost deserted. I found my place among the books and magazines, picking up the most recent edition of *Time.*

I felt excited as I absent-mindedly flipped through the magazine.

Finals week was about to begin, which meant school would be over soon and I could finally breathe again. The school year had been exhausting as I struggled just to make it through each day. I felt like my friends from freshman year had faded away and now, by the end of sophomore year, I was wondering who my friends were. Many students seemed uncomfortable around me, averting their eyes and getting noticeably quiet whenever I approached. I was glad to escape these dynamics by entering the upcoming summer break.

"Hey, Sam!" My head turned just in time to see a teacher, Mrs. Allen, approaching. We had met several weeks before. Mrs. Allen was a history teacher in charge of distributing "Character Awards," a way for teachers to nominate students for displaying noble qualities. She had presented me with the award. Afterward, she told me that she knew of my story. I appreciated her kindness during our conversation. She was known for her bubbly personality and care for her students.

"What are you still doing here?" she said in her sing-song voice with a smile.

I told her I stayed to avoid the traffic. We exchanged small-talk before I admitted how I really felt. "It's been a hard year," I told her.

She nodded. "I know. At least the year is almost over," she said.

I agreed and walked with her through the open doors of the school, into the now mostly-empty parking lot. We talked about the accident, and she empathized with how challenging the experience had been for me and my family.

Before we parted ways, she smiled at me and said, "It makes you who you are, right?"

Caught off guard, I tried to formulate an appropriate response. "Yes," I mumbled, nodding my head as I jumped into my car. I paused to consider her words. *Maybe this does make me who I am,* I thought. *But is this who I want to be?*

Leaning my head out of my lowered window, I attempted to offer this response to her, but she was already gone, driving down the winding road away from the school. I was left to wrestle once again with the implications of losing my face.

I KNOW WHY

Ignorance is bliss.
—Unknown

A bloodcurdling scream emerged from a brunette child with striking blue eyes. The child—one of my campers at a week-long summer camp—continued to scream relentlessly. We stood in a museum as part of a tour group arranged around a kindly docent who had just begun explaining the controls of an airplane. My camper, Bryce, continued to scream. "Ow," the docent exclaimed in response to Bryce's ill-timed disruptions. The others in our tour group looked uncomfortable.

I coaxed Bryce out of the simulated cockpit and led him toward the planes hanging in the middle of the museum, trying to quell his screams. I was Bryce's counselor for the summer camp serving children with special needs and their families. I had chosen to work at this camp as a way to give back. I was trying to get outside of my own head after the accident by being a part of something bigger than myself. Bryce had been diagnosed with autism, but was highly functioning and able to participate in nearly all activities successfully.

In my attempt to calm him, Bryce and I continued walking around the hanging planes. No luck. He continued to shriek, yelling his way through the museum. No words came out when he opened his mouth—he repeated his long, spine-tingling howl at an extremely high decibel. I led him from exhibit to exhibit, hoping that the change in scenery would reorient him. His screaming continued. I tried everything in my arsenal to calm him down. I gently asked him what was wrong, trying to see if we could fix whatever it was he found so upsetting. He remained unreachable. It was as if he was inhabiting another world, the intensity of his swirling emotions blocking out all other external stimuli.

After many unsuccessful attempts to calm him down, I asked if he wanted to leave. "NO!" he screamed. By this point, we had traveled to the front of the museum, safely away from causing further disturbances to those visiting the exhibits. I leaned down to talk with him, attempting to meet him where he was. I looked deep into Bryce's eyes to see if I could detect the source of his irritation. He looked sad and a little angry. It was like he wanted to cry out to the world, letting everyone know of his internal anguish.

I knew that everywhere he went Bryce was often told to be quiet. To behave. People often responded to him with critical looks, harsh stares, and judgment. It was part of his daily experience. I wanted to act differently, to treat him with the respect and understanding he deserved; to remind him of his value and place in this world.

The discomfort of others notwithstanding, I let him scream. We walked back to the main hall and wandered through the rest of the museum, visiting whichever exhibits he wanted to view. I asked him to lower his voice along the way and did my best to avoid security at every turn so as to avoid getting ejected from the museum.

Hours later, we left the museum, traveling to Chuck E. Cheese. Our arrival prompted a change in Bryce's behavior, and his smile reappeared as he played a myriad of games. Upon our return to camp, our exhausting day finally neared an end. Before returning inside, our group took a walk near the grounds on a path lined with trees and beautiful foliage. At first, we trekked along silently, taking in the scenery and enjoying the warm July weather. Bryce was the first to break the silence.

"Why was I screaming?" he asked.

"Well, I think you were upset about something," I answered.

A confused look came across his face. It was like the wheels of his mind started churning as he puzzled through his anger. "Well, do you know what I was angry about?" he asked me.

I thought about his question for a moment, trying to determine an appropriate answer. I couldn't pretend to understand or accurately capture the feelings he was experiencing, but my own experience came into my mind—the deep frustration I felt when others tried to tell me how to feel. I wanted to give him the answer he was looking for, an answer that could satisfy his curiosity and help him understand.

"Well, I don't think you liked the museum because there were so many people so close to you, but I think you are happier now, and maybe next time, you can tell me what is bothering you instead of screaming." I said.

Bryce nodded. My answer seemed to placate him.

"Yeah, I guess so," he replied.

Weeks later, as we neared the end of camp, the director facilitated a discussion among that summer's counselors. This served as an opportunity for us to debrief as a staff while sharing the lessons we had learned as a result of the experience. When my turn came, I told the story of Bryce at the museum and shared my thoughts. I felt blessed by my time with Bryce. He taught me something about my own experience over the past year and about my own relationship to my memory and the memory of my trauma.

"I know why I am angry," I said to the group. "Bryce didn't know why; he was angry for reasons that were entirely not his fault." Some say that ignorance is bliss, but I saw firsthand that an inability to understand the reason behind a feeling could have a frightening effect. For Bryce, it was a loss of control.

I had spent the last year bemoaning my memory. I had longed to forget, to be free from wrestling with the memories of my trauma. My memories had kept me up late into the night, tormented me during nearly every waking moment, and caused me to question nearly every aspect of my existence. I would have given almost anything to be able to forget, even just for a few minutes. Until spending time with Bryce helped me feel grateful again for the memory that I had once loved.

THE TRUTH COMES OUT

Truth is the torch that gleams through
the fog without dispelling it.
—Claude Adrien Helvetius

I pulled my car in front of a large townhouse in an unfamiliar neighborhood. Turning off the engine, I walked toward the front door, contemplating my list of questions I had prepared. I was on assignment, writing a story for a local newspaper about a member of the community.

After a few knocks, a man answered, opening the door only halfway. I could not see his face as he launched into a long monologue detailing both his accomplishments and exploits, bragging that his work helped save the country from destruction on many occasions. In his telling, the work he carried out was of the utmost importance to the nation, trickling out and impacting countries around the world.

I probed deeper still, inquiring about his upbringing. He helped me fill in the gaps, providing a dense, biographical outline of his life.

The man's long-winded answers revealed that he was clearly reveling in all of this newfound attention. For my part, I wanted to know everything about this mysterious man. Throughout the conversation, I attempted to ascertain the motivations behind this middle-aged man's every action, straining to sift through the morals and values that helped inform his existence.

The man kept talking, unaware that I had a question tucked away for safekeeping—one that I had been waiting several years to ask, a query that would likely shock the unsuspecting man to his core.

I waited for just the right moment to ask the question, hoping an element of surprise would work in my favor.

"Is it true that you were once responsible for the burning of a minor?"

The question hung in the air as silence fell over the conversation.

"Well, it wasn't my fault," the man said after a pregnant pause. "It was the woman's fault. It was her house. How was I supposed to know the acid was in her shed?"

I reminded the man of the allegation that he transported the minor to that specific location. Doesn't he possess any culpability?

The man continued to make the same claim that he wasn't responsible at all until I pushed the door fully open so he could see my face.

As soon as the man realized what was happening, he began to cry, sobbing loudly. I started crying, too.

"I didn't mean to. I really didn't. I didn't want that to happen," he said over and over.

With that, I turned away from the door and walked back to my car. I had gotten what I needed: an admission of guilt.

I drove away, leaving the man behind me. For the first time since the accident, I felt an overwhelming sense of peace. Moments later, I awoke.

If only life could unfold as artfully as it does in dreams.

THE ANNIVERSARY OF SEPTEMBER 1

The greatest test of courage on Earth is to
bear defeat without losing heart.
—Robert Green Ingersoll

As the first anniversary of the accident approached, I felt a sense of dread. Throughout the month of August, my irritability increased, as did my negative thoughts and feelings. It was as if my body could sense the upcoming milestone, and my emotions were ramping up in response.

My mother anticipated my reaction to this approaching date and responded accordingly. After much thought and conversation, we decided to redefine the day. We determined that September 1 would be a day of both remembrance and celebration, a day to prove that life goes on.

The preservation of my life was to be commemorated through an activity in which the whole family could participate. At first, I struggled to formulate an effective plan for the day. After all, what could we do to commemorate a day that changed the course of my life forever? I chose to go out to dinner.

We went to Morton's, a restaurant known for its legendary steaks. As we sat down at the table, a waitress came over to us and asked, "Are you celebrating a birthday?"

"A celebration of life," my mother said.

The waitress looked confused. She changed the topic, talking about steak options for the evening. My family and I engaged in silly, jovial banter, as we typically do, through the rest of the dinner. We each went around the table and shared reflections from the past year, as well as words of encouragement.

Before ordering dessert, my mother asked the waitress to take a photo of us. I usually cringed when the camera appeared, but on this night, I agreed. This query prompted the waitress to ask again about the reason for our celebration. "Our oldest was in an accident a year ago," my mother said, pointing to me.

"Oh, a car accident?" the waitress asked.

I explained that it was an accident with sulfuric acid.

The waitress looked troubled. She quickly segued to the dessert menu and left shortly thereafter.

Looking around the table that night, I realized the importance of holding my family close. They were the ones who had been there for me every step of the way. When so many others had left, my family had remained, loving me through the overwhelming physical, emotional and spiritual pain from the last year.

As we left the restaurant, we walked around in the cool night air and resolved to carry out a similar celebration the following year. This night gave birth to what would become an annual tradition that would help sustain me in the weeks, months, and years ahead: acknowledging the pain of my experience, while celebrating all we had achieved in my healing. Even as despondent as I felt on most days, I always had the love of my family. And that was worth celebrating, whether or not September 1 had rolled around.

BEHIND ENEMY LINES

Keep your friends close, and your enemies closer.
—Sun Tzu, *The Art of War*

After a summer that felt too short, junior year began. It was mid-September, and a new school year offered an opportunity to look toward the future. I developed a robust list of potential colleges to explore and made plans to visit a few of them along the East Coast. My first college visit happened to coincide with Election Day, ensuring a quick stop at the polls for my mother to cast her ballot before we proceeded on our drive to the University of Mary Washington.

We were eager to leave for our college adventure, so my mother, sister, and I arrived at the polls early that morning. We pulled into the parking of my high school, which doubled as a polling station. Suddenly, a look of horror crossed my mother's face. She had caught sight of something. My mother gently placed her hand on mine and motioned toward the front of the school.

I looked, searching for what she was pointing at. I noticed a man passing out flyers in front of the building. I almost didn't recognize him. It was the man who had hired me for the neighborhood job on that fateful September day. My heart started racing. *Why was he here?* I wondered.

I had heard through the grapevine that he had moved out of the county so I thought our paths would never cross again. I certainly did not expect to encounter him again in this way. His presence so close to my school and home was unsettling. I felt paralyzed as I sat in the car, attempting to forge a plan to avoid interacting with him.

"Should we even walk in?" my mother asked.

"Yes," I said calmly, regaining my composure. I was determined— our lives had already been altered enough by this man. I resolved to walk into the polling station with my head held high. "He won't recognize me anyway," I told my mother, hoping that my prediction would be correct.

I walked toward the school confidently and calmly. As I neared the man, my heart began to pound. He stood in between the sidewalk and the front door, requiring that I walk past him in order to get into the building. I approached him, trying to conceal my nerves. He made the first move, extending his arm with a flier on behalf of a candidate. I looked directly into his eyes to see if he'd recognize me.

The world slowed down as our eyes locked. I wondered if there was more to this man than I had once observed. If only I could read his motives. Perhaps, if I understood him, I could feel a sense of healing.

The confrontation was anticlimactic. He showed no signs of recognizing me. After a few seconds, we pressed on, moving toward the doors of my high school. There were more pressing matters to attend to; votes to cast, colleges to see. My earlier prediction rang true: He didn't recognize me. I was invisible even to my own aggressor.

As we stood in line to vote, I wished that the man had recognized me. I will always remember his face—it's the face that changed my life—but only a year and two months after the accident, he had already forgotten mine. I grimaced at the thought of him sleeping peacefully each night while I lay awake, tormented by his face, his garage, and his belongings.

A few days later, I was still wrestling with the implications of this unexpected encounter. I was sharing my story with a group of students in a class called Positive Experiences in Educational Relationships (PEER). We were a group of sixteen students who had been selected to provide mentorship to students within our school, as well as at a nearby middle school. Every other week, we had a designated class period for students to share personal reflections. Oftentimes, the group would respond with thoughts or feedback.

"Maybe this was the moment you needed in order to heal," Mrs. Kaplan, the guidance counselor, said to me. She was referring to my encounter with the man outside of the polling place.

Her words caught me off guard. For a moment, I believed her. Maybe my confrontation, or lack thereof, with the man would be enough to push me toward some semblance of healing.

OH, WHAT LASERS CAN DO

When you pass through the waters, I will be with you;
and through the rivers, they shall not overwhelm
you; when you walk through fire you shall not be
burned, and the flame shall not consume you.
—Isaiah 43:2

In a follow-up appointment with Dr. Randall, he examined my scars and recommended laser treatments. At this point, I was most concerned about the scars under my nose, forehead, and chin. The skin graft placed under my nose had done little to decrease the visibility of the scar. I felt it looked even worse than it had before the surgery. My "Harry Potter" scar—the one on my forehead—had been slightly reduced in size, yet the redness was still present. My chin continued to look like someone had taken a bite out of it and red marks were still splayed across my neck.

Dr. Randall decided that applying a laser to my scars would reduce their appearance by decreasing the level of redness surrounding each scar. Relieved at the thought of not having to undergo another full-length surgery, I agreed to this round of treatment.

It was difficult to make an appointment for the laser procedure. The office shared a laser with other providers, meaning that they only had access to the laser a few times a month. As a result, appointment times were challenging to secure. After scheduling an appointment well in advance, the doctor's office contacted me the day before the procedure to say that the laser would not be in Dr. Randall's office as previously scheduled. My mother rescheduled the appointment, chalking this up to one of life's unanticipated setbacks.

When the exact same scenario played out again directly before the second appointment, this turn of events felt more than coincidental. This was confirmed in the weeks following when the office failed to contact us again, despite my mother's repeated calls. I felt rejected by Dr. Randall and a bit confused by his office's inability to schedule me for a follow-up appointment. In light of these scheduling difficulties, we decided to find a new doctor.

Shortly afterward, I was telling a friend at church about my experience with plastic surgeons. Upon hearing my story, my friend recommended a medical professional named Bill Hobbs. In an email a few days after our conversation, my friend wrote, "He does non-surgical cosmetic work, mostly with lasers. He is a good friend and great doctor." His words made this doctor sound promising.

Soon after, I scheduled an appointment and met with Mr. Hobbs for more than an hour. Mr. Hobbs was willing to listen and had a kind demeanor that intrigued me. He was balding, with a toothy smile and glasses, and had an incredible ability to focus on me when I was speaking. He never wavered or averted his gaze. He remained engaged as my mother and I took turns telling my story. As the story unfolded,

Mr. Hobbs looked distraught. He was dressed in blue scrubs and sat on a rolling chair. He wrapped his arms around his stomach, as if he was about to be sick. Ever-so-slightly, he rocked back and forth.

Before the end of my appointment, he asked a few questions in a soft voice. He had a degree in nursing with nearly twenty years of experience and a deep understanding of lasers and possible treatments. He appeared confident that laser treatment would do much good in the fight to reduce my scars.

Mr. Hobbs tried to prepare me for what the first session would entail. Everyone reacts differently to the lasers, he explained, so it was hard to predict how I would respond. Our sessions required that I wear a pair of sunglasses to protect my eyesight. As a result, I never saw the laser zapping my skin, nor was I ever able to anticipate what part of my body would feel the laser next. Whoever accompanied me was also required to wear protective eyewear, although they were able to still see.

I was instructed to dress in all black clothing for each session, I assumed because bright colored clothing would somehow counteract the lasers. I would hear the whirring of the laser as Mr. Hobbs turned on the machine, my eyewear preventing me from watching as he brought the end of the laser close to my face. Bringing the laser down to my scars, he would zap the area, as if I had just come into contact with an electrical socket. The bolt of electricity would provide a jolt to my body, causing my whole frame to react by jumping in the chair. Once I resumed my original posture of lying down, I could detect the strong, pungent smell of burning skin. Before long, Mr. Hobbs was at it again, focusing on a different area and using his laser to poke small holes in the scars. Memories came flooding back. The burning sensation caused by the laser felt eerily similar to the feeling of being burned alive nearly two years before.

I recognized that these sessions were triggering my PTSD symptoms. As I sat in the patient's chair, my fight or flight reaction increased, including heightened breathing and rising anxiety. In addition to my escalating emotions, the pain was nearly unbearable. At times, it felt like someone was taking a knife to my face and cutting my skin open. Sometimes, I felt like I was on the other end of a plug placed into the wrong electrical socket, experiencing repeated unwanted jolts to my face. Unlike other surgical procedures, I was not under anesthesia, nor was I given anything to numb the pain.

I kept calm by reminding myself that this was different from the accident. I ran over the facts—as he described it, Mr. Hobbs was using the laser to drill small, concentrated holes to help reduce the size of my scars. To cope, I grabbed my mother's hand, holding onto her as the laser made its way across my face and arms.

He would idly talk as the treatment was underway, sharing stories of his time in Pittsburgh (where he grew up and went to college), as well as his adventures in the military while completing his residency at an Army Medical Center. He talked about his mother and his children, especially his son.

He also discussed other patients, regaling us with wild stories. He shared funny anecdotes from his encounters, such as the moms wanting to look much younger than their true ages and the wealthy women trying to improve their odds of landing younger men.

To his credit, Mr. Hobbs said he needed to calibrate the lasers at a much higher rate than he would typically for his other patients, I assumed because operating on my scars required more aggression than on undamaged skin. He said that as treatment progressed, he would need to continue increasing the calibration. Every few weeks, I would undergo a higher intensity of treatment than in the previous appointment.

"I'm turning it up to kill levels," Mr. Hobbs declared half-jokingly as our sessions progressed, turning the laser calibration ever higher. He did his best to smile and laugh up until the moment I put my glasses on when I no longer could read his facial expressions. After the procedure, I pulled off my glasses and could sometimes detect a hint of emotion in his eyes.

On the car ride home, my mother would fill me in on all she observed during the session. She told me of the moments when he looked at her with tears in his eyes, turning his head away as if he could no longer look at my still burning face.

Laser operations are normally quite costly. These laser procedures were not covered under my parents' insurance plan and would cost upwards of several thousand dollars. We were surprised after the first few sessions when the bill was much smaller. When my mother thanked him, he brushed it aside, saying he was, "happy to offer a discount."

Before each treatment, Mr. Hobbs took pictures to track my progress by comparing before and after images. Over the course of nearly a year, the assembled photos showed little visible progress. The skin graft under my nose appeared unchanged, and my nose continued to collapse, making it increasingly difficult to breathe out of my right nostril. Little progress had been made in reducing the redness of the scars on my forehead, chin, and neck. The laser was proving ineffective.

Mr. Hobbs seemed surprised by this turn of events as he reviewed the assembled photos with my mother and me. He expressed concern over the state of my nose and pointed out that the laser was unable to prevent the scar under my nose from applying further pressure to my right nostril.

As a result, Mr. Hobbs recommended we find a surgical solution— something more significant and aggressive than he could do himself. Once again, my mother and I began searching for a plastic surgeon, but I was filled with gratefulness to have encountered Mr. Hobbs in all of his goodness and kindness.

PLAYING WITH FIRE

The unexamined life is not worth living.
—Socrates

A Google search led us to Dr. Wang, a well-regarded plastic surgeon in Northern Virginia.

Upon learning about my laser treatments with Mr. Hobbs, this new surgeon asked if the laser had been directed at the skin graft under my nose. "Yes," I answered.

"Interesting," he said with a look of concern. "Lasers are not meant to correct skin grafts."

Apparently, using a laser to break up skin grafts was not effective.

I was shaken. The pain I endured from that laser on the skin graft under my nose had all been a waste. I felt betrayed and disappointed.

Dr. Wang continued talking with us, offering extended explanations about the intricacies of plastic surgery. At one point, he asked to see pictures from right after the accident so that he could assess the level of damage from the initial injuries. The minute he saw the images, he grimaced. His face contorted into a frown as he turned his head to the side to examine the photos.

Dr. Wang's depth of knowledge, paired with his straight answers, was appealing. He recommended that we schedule surgery as quickly as possible. He felt confident he could easily correct my chin, by being "more creative," he said.

I wondered what that meant.

In reference to the upcoming operation, he outlined his surgical approach. "I like to play," Dr. Wang said mischievously, smiling as he uttered the words. Looking out the window of his office toward the line of trees, I tried to process his statement. *When did my face become a playground?* I wondered.

Grabbing a mirror, Dr. Wang held it to my face and outlined the incisions he planned to make, simulating the effects of the knife with his hand. Since the mirror was positioned so that only my mother could view his movements, I was left out of the process, unable to see the motions he made.

As the appointment came to a close, he indicated that we should make a follow-up appointment so that we could "go over a few things." I felt rushed, as if his singular focus was on getting me under the knife. This should have been expected, I presumed; after all, the man liked to play.

A TOUCH OF KINDNESS

Kindness is the language which the deaf
can hear and the blind can see.
—Mark Twain

Weeks later, I found myself yet again in the office of a new plastic surgeon.

Dr. Michaels was a tall man with dark hair and a skinny waist, with a deep intensity in his eyes. He spoke carefully, as if he was measuring each word before it left his mouth. He looked at me inquisitively, keeping his eyes trained on me for most of the appointment. Despite the serious look on his face, he exuded kindness. He had a gentle and strong presence.

He began the appointment by inspecting every inch of my face. He observed, saying very little as he slid my head around with his hands in an effort to gain a better look. I felt like a museum piece, on display to see and touch.

The doctor said, "I am sorry to poke and prod you. I am sure that is not what you want."

Once his inspection was complete, he retrieved a camera from a cabinet. He positioned the camera a few inches from my face, eliciting a sense of dread on my part. Since the first few days after the accident, my disdain for cameras grew, so much so that I began to actively avoid having my picture taken. Cameras were the enemy, tending to make me feel insecure and self-conscious about my appearance.

But it was deeper than that. Cameras felt invasive, capturing my scars and preserving them in an image in a way that I didn't want. I was not interested in preserving any pictures of my face or remembering it in this way. I didn't want to be reminded of the most traumatic day of my life. It also felt too personal for others to see my face this way—even if they were just doctors and medical staff.

Perhaps sensing my discomfort, Dr. Michaels broke the silence by saying, "Sorry to get up in your face and to be so invasive." His body language looked heavy as he placed his thumb on the camera, gingerly capturing the shot.

After the last picture was taken, he outlined his plan. He grabbed a Q-Tip, waving the object around the areas where he planned to operate. He said the scars on my chin and neck were "very wide," and that he could narrow their width, while also repairing the uncomfortable graft directly under my nose.

He also planned to remove the graft and create a new scar in its place, one that would travel along the top of my lip.

He explained that this would reduce pressure on my nose and, after a few months, the new scar would hardly be noticeable.

"Will I be able to grow facial hair?" I asked.

"Growing facial hair would definitely be a good option," he said. "My goal, however, is to eliminate the need for facial hair—you won't feel the need to hide any scars, because they will be barely noticeable," he said.

Samuel Moore-Sobel

He answered my remaining questions, careful to explore all options before making a final decision. Over the course of the appointment, his methodical approach and willingness to engage earned my trust.

He wished us well as we left. Moving towards the exit, I looked back one last time. Dr. Michaels had retreated to his office, standing tall as he viewed the titles of books on his shelves, scanning as if he had a title in mind. He carefully pulled out a large, impressive-looking book before diving into the material. The research was underway.

MAYBE GERVAIS WAS RIGHT

Sir, why did you take such pains to hide yourself?
—Bertrand Russell

"What, because I'm saying I don't believe in God?" Ricky Gervais said.

Sitting in my parents' bedroom, I was watching as British comedian Ricky Gervais was being interviewed by Piers Morgan on CNN. Just before bed, I was doing my best to decompress, hoping that I would fall into a peaceful sleep. Morgan was pressing Gervais on his religious beliefs, and Gervais was answering Morgan's questions as if he was simply stating the obvious. I was struck by his sense of freedom about his beliefs (or lack thereof). He appeared so unencumbered, released from the demands of a religious life. He appeared to be free from guilt and shame, able to live as he pleased.

I could not help but be drawn to his confidence. After a few minutes, I stopped watching the television and walked towards my room. *What if there is no God?* I wondered. *Was it possible that everything I was taught in my evangelical upbringing was merely a clever farce? What if the very foundation upon which my life has been built was wrong?* I wondered.

Climbing into bed, a part of me longed for the words uttered by the charismatic comedian to ring true. *If God did not exist, life would be simpler*, I thought. Then, the question I often grappled with—why bad things happened—would be irrelevant. Ever since the accident, I had wrestled with that concept. If God controls all things, then why did He allow my face to be burned? Or, was He unable to intervene, constrained by a lack of supernatural power when it comes to combatting evil? These were the only two options that made sense to me based upon my experience and I found both to be extremely troubling.

But then I would think about how my eyes were preserved in the accident. How every doctor said I should have died or, at least, lost my eyesight. They couldn't explain it. It was a miracle. This was just one way that I felt God's presence in my life. I had spent years studying my faith and learning about other faith traditions, at times actively searching for an alternative. Yet none could satisfy my intellectual, emotional, physical and spiritual needs in the way that my belief in Christ could.

I laid awake in my bed that night pondering Ricky Gervais' words. I felt stuck between what I knew to be true and the conflicting desires of my heart. Vacillating between the two, my wrestling only came to an end once my eyes shut and I finally drifted off to sleep.

CONTENDING FOR MORE

Then he said, 'Your name shall no longer be
called Jacob, but Israel, for you have striven with
God and with men, and have prevailed.'
—Genesis 32:28

"You know the story of Jacob?" I asked.

Dr. Leo, my psychiatrist, was sitting across from me, looking at me intently. In these moments, I felt his intelligence and care for me. He looked stoic, but his eyes held sensitivity and compassion. He was perceptive, always able to detect when I was hedging or trying to deflect. After so many sessions, he must have learned my patterns. He had to know how this particular conversation would end.

"The story of Jacob?" he asked.

"Yeah, the story of Jacob wrestling the angel."

"Ah," he said, nodding.

In this story from the book of Genesis, Jacob encounters a man and wrestles with him through the night. He refuses to let the man go until he receives a "blessing." The man blesses him, changing Jacob's name to Israel. While there is some debate as to the identity of the man, he is believed to have been some sort of heavenly creature.

"He gets the blessing in the end," Dr. Leo said as I continued in my recollection of the story, as if trying to nudge me towards the happy ending.

"Yes, but he struggles," I said.

"But he gets the blessing," Dr. Leo said again.

"I feel like Jacob wrestling with the angel," I finally admitted, even though it was obvious Dr. Leo already knew this without my saying it. Since the acid first hit my face, I had been engaged in a struggle with the God I was taught to love. I was unsure of how to trust Him after all that had happened to me. I shifted my gaze to the ground as if I was suddenly interested in the couch fabric.

"So, when are you gonna stop wrestling?" Dr. Leo asked, smiling as he awaited my response.

"I don't know," I said.

Sometime later, I told my friend Ethan about this conversation. At that time, Ethan was in seminary. He knew a lot about God and religion. We had talked about topics of faith often.

In my conversation with Ethan, I bemoaned my inability to stop wrestling. I articulated my desire to emulate the faith of many around me. I admired their ability to weather the waves of life without any semblance of disbelief. Unlike them, my faith felt strong one moment and fragile the next.

"You never left," he said, referring to the fact that I had chosen not to leave my faith behind. "You may still wrestle, but you never left."

It was like he knew. I couldn't leave my faith behind. Not while I, like Jacob, was in the midst of waiting for the blessing.

DISORIENTATION

A fair face may be a foul bargain.
—Unknown

Over Christmas break of my junior year, I found myself back in the hospital for another scar revision surgery.

The anesthesiologist began by detailing the risks of undergoing anesthesia, including pneumonia.

"I don't want to do any of that today," he said.

"Neither do I," I responded.

The doctor continued, laying out additional risks. The list continued to expand, only heightening my feelings of insecurity. After a few moments, I began to zone out, overwhelmed by all that could go wrong.

As the anesthesiologist left, as if on cue, my plastic surgeon, Dr. Michaels, arrived. Just as he had in our previous appointments, a serious look encompassed his face as he began his pre-surgery routine. I could feel the weight of his strong, calming presence the moment he strode through the open door. He started off by inspecting my face. His brow furrowed the moment he saw the mark under my nose made by the attending nurse. She had done so to highlight the part of my body on which the doctor would be operating. "I don't know why they did that," he said in an irritated tone. He immediately handed me a cloth so that I could wipe my nose clean.

Next, Dr. Michaels handed me a clipboard containing what felt like the hundredth consent form I had signed that morning. This was the typical pre-surgery legal form releasing the doctor from liability. Once I had signed the bottom of the page, the doctor had one last order of business.

In his hands was a large, bound book filled with the surgical results of previous patients. Flipping through the book as if looking for a specific patient, he landed on a page featuring the before and after pictures of an operation. The patient in the images had faced similar circumstances to mine—her face had been disfigured in a traumatic event. In the picture taken before the surgery, the scars surrounding her nose looked much like mine: red, large, and uncomfortable. The picture taken after the operation revealed a remarkable difference. The woman's nose looked brand new, the redness almost completely eradicated as a result of Dr. Michaels's handiwork.

Seeing this picture calmed my nerves and reinforced the reason behind my decision to undergo another operation. I could not help but hope that this surgery could produce an outcome close to the one I saw in the pictures.

"Do you smoke?" Dr. Michaels asked.

"No," I said.

"Good," he said, with a satisfied look upon his face. "Smoking is a nasty habit. Never start. Any questions?"

"No," I said haltingly.

"You will be fine," he said confidently, turning around and promptly striding out of the room.

———

A short while after the end of Dr. Michaels' visit, the nurses wheeled me down the halls into the operating room. My nerves began to steadily rise. Transferring me from the gurney onto the operating table, I suddenly had a change of heart.

I don't want to do this again, I thought to myself. I ran through the list of risks outlined by the anesthesiologist. Suddenly, in this setting, his words felt all the more real. Turning toward the nurses, I leaned over the table, doing my best to assess the room. Just then, one of the nurses placed a clear mask over my face before I could utter even a sound. Within seconds my eyes closed, and I descended into a peaceful slumber.

———

After the surgery, I had just one question.

"How do I look?" I asked the nurse standing nearby.

"You look good," he said.

"How long was I in surgery?" I asked.

"You had surgery from twelve fifteen to three o'clock."

"When did I wake up?"

"Three thirty. "

Suddenly, I realized that my bladder felt like it would explode.

"I need to go to the bathroom," I said.

Dutifully, the male nurse came up beside me in an effort to help me relieve myself. Wearing blue scrubs, he smiled as he placed his arms around me to help me to my feet. Still feeling groggy, I struggled as I attempted to exit the bed. It felt as if my brain was commanding my legs to move, yet my lower limbs were unable to carry out the request. Slowly, I sat up. The blood rushed to my head, making me feel dizzy.

Finally, I made it to the bathroom and successfully relieved myself. Approaching the sink, I turned on the cool water. My eyes remained trained on my hands as I washed them. I felt unready to lift my gaze to the mirror. Upon returning to bed, the nurse struck up a conversation with me.

"Did you look in the mirror?" he asked.

"No," I said.

"Hmm," he said with a surprised look in his eyes.

Maybe I would have the nerve to look at myself next time.

POST-SURGERY BLISS

In the time of darkest defeat, victory may be nearest.
—William McKinley

The first few days after surgery were a blur.

I was in immense pain, and I felt lethargic and emotionally distant, similar to what I had experienced after previous operations. My parents, brother, and sister kept careful watch over me, encouraging me to conserve my energy.

Stitches and sutures were protruding from my face, encased by a yellow, packed bandage hanging over my upper lip. I was instructed by the doctor to keep the area moist with antibiotic cream. Due to the large bandages, stitches and sutures, I was unable to move my upper lip, much less blow my nose. I longed for my appointment seven days later when the stitches would be removed.

With my constrained ability to chew, my diet was limited to lots of pudding, Jell-O, and soup. I wore button down shirts per the doctor's instruction so that I didn't pull out any stiches when taking off my shirt. I relied on my family, unable to shower on my own.

A few days after my surgery, my family and I watched as the New Orleans Saints took on the Atlanta Falcons. It was the day after Christmas, and we were all excited to be spending time together. My father was rooting for Drew Brees, the quarterback of the Saints, and naturally, I was, too. History stood to be made on that night—Drew Brees was closing in on the single-season passing record held by Dan Marino, the legendary quarterback of the Miami Dolphins. Everyone in the family was watching expectantly—even my mother, who normally avoided professional sports.

We watched in awe as Brees set the new single-season passing record, effortlessly lobbing the ball across the field during the entire game. After the game, Brees was standing in front of the television cameras for the requisite interview. Before he started talking, I noticed something about his appearance. Walking closer toward the television to get a better look, I saw a giant birthmark on his right cheek. A brown mark just underneath his right eye which was visible whenever he smiled.

His words were not the most memorable part of the experience. Watching him stand so confidently in front of cameras that were beaming him into millions of homes across America, I could not help but wonder about Brees' confidence. *What about the birthmark?* I wondered. *How did that not hamper his ability to be successful?*

Later that night I purchased his autobiography, reading the first few chapters on my Kindle in an effort to find an answer to my question. Brees seemed to be proud of his birthmark. In fact, he made it clear that he would never remove the mark on his face because it was a part of him that he never wanted to lose.

I was struck by his words. I constantly wanted to be free from my scars. I marveled at Brees' ability to make peace with the part of himself that he had chosen never to remove. I had spent the last few years striving for others to accept and affirm my face, but perhaps I needed to simply find acceptance from myself.

After Brees' interview, I couldn't help but wonder: Could I, too, set records and achieve victories in spite of the marks on my face?

STITCHES NO MORE

*The best and most beautiful things in the world cannot be
seen or even touched—they must be felt with the heart.*
—Helen Keller

I nearly leapt out of bed on the day my stitches were to be removed.
I was so excited to finally be free of them.

At the office, the doctor examined my face, saying that the scars
were healing well. Using a tool that looked like tweezers, he began to
whittle away at the stitches under my nose. Bracing myself for extreme
pain, I was pleasantly surprised when I only felt mild discomfort. Yet
the joy I felt over the lack of pain quickly evaporated when I looked
at my new face for the first time.

My face was swollen and red, which was to be expected. I knew
the swelling and redness would recede with time. All of the scars on
my face appeared elevated, and it looked like I had been beaten up.

While I detected an improvement in the appearance of my nose, I immediately noticed that a freshly-cut scar now ran along the right side of my face. It started at the base of my right nostril and cascaded down, connecting with the scar on my upper lip. The scar appeared to take up a larger part of my face than the skin graft that had been under my nose before the operation, and I wondered if others would be able to readily detect this newly created scar. *Wasn't the point of the surgery to reduce my scars?* I wondered.

WHAT DO YOU THINK?

Everyday courage has few witnesses. But yours is no less noble because no drum beats for you and no crowds shout your name.
—Robert Louis Stevenson

Acclimating to life after surgery was not an easy task. My return to school after the holiday break was no different. My brain still felt groggy and my continued pain and soreness made me feel as if my body was in a different place than my mind. Nevertheless, I entered the classroom with a smile. Sometimes, pretending was the only way to survive.

My first class of the day was PEER, the one taught by Mrs. Allen. The class was lively, filled with a cast of characters who always had something to say. On any given day, students were usually milling about, talking hurriedly about their lives. The girls were in the corner obsessing over Madison's new relationship. "I don't want to talk about this," she would say before invariably divulging details. Chase was obsessing over how he had done on his most recent test, and Michael had a penchant for talking about his last lacrosse game. Most were excited to be there, feeling safe in the environment Mrs. Allen had fostered.

On this day, I could hear the typical hum of movement and conversation in the room. That is, until the moment my foot crossed the threshold of the classroom. Immediately, silence fell over the group. Everyone stared at me. I suppose my new appearance was not one they had expected.

"Your beard is fierce, man!" one of my classmates yelled out in a fit of testosterone. Other classmates approached me, hovering to offer their own assessments of my change in appearance.

"Hey nice mustache. That was the fir—" my friend Chase said, before stopping himself to look down at the ground for a brief moment. "Second thing I noticed. I won't B.S. you, I noticed your face first," he said. He embraced me in a big hug. His words soothed the butterflies I felt in my stomach.

Minutes later, another classmate approached. She said, "Honestly, I don't think they should have cut you up. You looked better before."

I understood what she meant and agreed with her. I myself was having trouble getting accustomed to my new appearance. I spent time looking in the mirror each morning, hoping and praying that the swelling would recede with each passing day.

Reactions to my new face were mixed. Some were pleased with the surgery while others didn't understand why I kept going to the doctor. Some were quick to provide advice while others opted to stay quiet, their true thoughts only detectable when I looked them in the eye or observed a change in their body language.

Days later I visited my father at his office. A quiet, older accountant worked in the same office building as my father. I always tried to grab a few moments with the accountant whenever I visited, eager to talk to the friendly man whom I had grown to respect. I trusted his opinion and, more importantly, his words. He knew about my surgery and did his best to encourage my father in the days after my procedure.

"How do I look?" I asked him nervously.

"I like the beard," he said. "It is an improvement. I think your face doesn't look all that bad."

"Yeah, but the scars are red and now my face is swollen," I said.

"Yeah, those were all things that they told you before the surgery, right? You knew it wouldn't look perfect right away," he told me gently.

To his credit, Dr. Michaels had explained everything before the surgery. Oftentimes, he had said, surgery makes the treated area look worse in the initial stages of healing.

At the time, I had understood what Dr. Michaels said and willingly accepted it. But now that the warning had become my reality, I struggled to embrace it. The dryness of my face, accompanied by my rapidly growing facial hair, only heightened my alarm and discomfort.

Unfortunately, the unwanted stares that were just beginning to lessen before the surgery, began again. People cocked their head as I walked by, attempting to catch a better glimpse of my swollen face. Some did a double take as I walked past them. To be fair, I understood that there was a lot to see: my face was red, much redder than the average person, and puffy, so it looked larger than it was and a bit inflated. My chin was raised, and one could still see the indents left by the stitches just taken out.

It was hard, though, to be the recipient of these stares. I reacted by pulling my hand over my face in an attempt to cover the scars under my nose. Often, I would rest my hand directly under my chin, attempting to camouflage the scar, or even to subtly redirect people's attention. My efforts to hide rarely worked.

During this time, I felt a deep need for the affirmation of others which created its own set of problems. Others often offered their opinions of my new face. This feedback weighed on me. If only I could be comfortable in my own skin. If only I had known then what I know now: that looking for reassurance from others can be a dangerous game because true healing comes from within.

WAKE-UP CALL

Difficult things take a long time,
impossible things a little longer.
—Unknown

"You are right where I want you to be," Dr. Michaels said at our next appointment.

I struggled to understand how this could be. I wasn't where I wanted to be. I remained perturbed by the new scar running down the right side of my face. A friend referred to this new scar as a "laugh line," pointing out that it disappeared whenever I smiled. But no one spends all their waking moments smiling. How was I supposed to hide my scar when a smile wasn't on my face?

"You're in a better global position now where we can excise and treat," Dr. Michaels began.

Did this mean more surgeries were ahead? I wondered. I had thought that this operation was going to be my last. I wasn't sure that I was up for another surgery. In fact, I was pretty determined that the surgeries and operations needed to come to an end. After nearly a year and a half, I was ready to call it quits. *How many more years of surgeries was I supposed to endure?* I wondered.

"Are you alarmed?" I asked Dr. Michaels. These were the first three words that popped into my head.

"No," he answered.

Unsatisfied, I asked him again. "Are you alarmed?"

"No," he said again.

Equally unsatisfied, I found a third way to ask my question again. He swerved around, looked me in the eye, and said with a hint of irritation, "I am not alarmed by it—are you?"

I wanted to tell him that yes, I was alarmed. I was alarmed every time I looked in the mirror and saw a new scar near my lip. I was alarmed every time I felt the scar under my right nostril become more constricted, worrying that one day it would just permanently close. I was alarmed to hear that more surgeries were to come and that additional years of my life might be overcome by the repercussions of an accident that had already stolen far too much.

But I didn't say any of that. I didn't know what to say.

In the days and weeks after my appointment with Dr. Michaels, I was convinced that another surgery was not a viable route. Emotionally, it was becoming too much for me to handle. I was stuck in what felt like a merry-go-round of never-ending tweaks to my face.

My tolerance for the doctors, the pain, the physical toll on my body, and the havoc on my emotions was waning. Looking in the mirror after an operation was hard. I felt unrecognizable, even to myself. I felt so little control over how my face would look once the doctor had finished with his knife. A part of me desperately hoped that if my face was finally left alone, the scars would naturally fade.

"This is my last surgery," I declared to my parents.

"You always say that," my mother said.

"I know," I responded. "But this time, I mean it."

A BOTTOMLESS PIT

For a man seldom thinks with more earnestness
of anything than he does of his dinner.
—Samuel Johnson, *Piozzi's Anecdotes of the Late Samuel Johnson*

"I never feel full," I told Dr. Leo in one of our sessions.

By this point, I had become noticeably overweight. I was filled with shame over my appearance and desired to be fitter, but I was hungry all the time and engaged in extended bouts of overeating.

That day, I decided to tell Dr. Leo my secret. For months, I had been making clandestine trips to the McDonald's a few minutes from my high school. Every time I approached the drive-through, I felt an internal battle rage. I would think about turning back, but my foot would press down on the accelerator and I'd inch forward. Then I would order my favorite snack: large fries and a hot fudge sundae. I'd scarf down the fries and dig my spoon into the sundae to satisfy my insatiable hunger.

I felt powerful each time I went to McDonald's. It was my secret. After finishing my meal and ridding myself of the evidence, I felt a wave of control. Doctors might tell me how to live, friends might make insensitive remarks, and my face might refuse to heal, but no one could tell me how to eat.

I gained a significant amount of weight. My weight gain was exacerbated by the strict limits on my ability to exercise. Doctors told me to avoid going outside for long periods of time because the sun could damage my scars. Sweating also irritated my scars, especially after surgeries. As a result, I refrained from most outdoor activities. All these factors meant that by the end of the school year, I had gained nearly fifty pounds.

I explained all of this to Dr. Leo. He sat in a plush chair near his desk, betraying no look of surprise.

"Do you think this relates to how you feel emotionally?" he asked.

"Maybe," I said.

I told him that I had felt this way even before the accident. No matter how much food I ate, it was never enough. No amount of food ever made me feel whole.

"Food does not have the power to make you feel whole," he said to me.

"But I don't feel full," I told him.

All I wanted was to finally feel full.

SOMEONE TO LOVE

I love you for all that you are, all that you
have been, and all that you will be.
—Unknown

I used to wonder what life would have been like for my family if I had died on September 1.

One day, I brought this topic up with my mother, wondering if she had ever considered what would have happened to her if I had died.

"If you had died, your father and I would have considered having another child," she said.

Stunned, I thought about what that would have meant for my siblings.

"I would have really struggled," she said. Her last pregnancy with my sister had been a hard one for her. Plus, she would have been almost forty, an age which might have dissuaded her from getting pregnant.

"We could have adopted," she said. "But your father would have wanted a biological child."

It felt strange discussing my hypothetical death with my mother. The idea of my parents having more children in the wake of my purely theoretical untimely demise was especially peculiar. Although it made sense to me that they would consider having another child.

"I wonder if you would have had another baby," I said.

"I'm glad I didn't have to find out," she said.

In my next session with Dr. Leo, I relayed this conversation.

"I always wanted my parents to have another child," I told Dr. Leo.

"Why?" Dr. Leo said.

"I don't know," I answered.

He let me fumble around with my thoughts for a bit longer. We had often talked about my feelings of loss due to the accident. I posited that my desire for a third sibling was somehow connected to losing my face.

"Why?" he said again, probing ever deeper.

"I don't know," I said. "Isn't that what I pay you for?"

He chuckled, and then answered. "Perhaps you wanted someone else to love."

The implication being that witnessing the beginning of a new life would somehow restore what I, along with my family, had lost. Growing up in a loving family, I had always wanted to add more to the mix. Certainly, gaining a fourth would have produced an even number of children, but, even more consequentially, having someone else to love would have provided me with the opportunity to pour into a young life. After spending the last few years feeling relegated to the sidelines, unable to fully function independently due to my health, my parents having another child would have garnered me the opportunity to feel needed. To have a second chance, as it were: a clean slate. To have a sibling who didn't know the difference between what my face looked like before I lost it. To have the opportunity to craft a whole new identity with a sibling who wouldn't know the difference between what I once looked like and my current appearance.

ARE WE DONE HERE?

Even the darkest night will end and the sun will rise.
—Victor Hugo, *Les Misérables*

Halfway through my junior year, I was still struggling with the intended purpose of the sulfuric acid. *Why had the sulfuric acid been so carelessly stored in that shed?* I perpetually wondered.

There was no shortage of theories posited by those around me. A family friend, who was an engineer by trade with a background in chemistry, often reminded my family and me of a theory he had developed in the years since the accident.

He believed that the sulfuric acid, located in a box and housed in a shed, had been used as an ingredient in the creation of illegal drugs. The concentration of the sulfuric acid, he believed, was far too high to support the woman's claims that her ex-husband had been using it for metal etching. At a concentration that high, the acid would have burned through the metal. This was a fact that doctors had repeatedly echoed in the years since by saying that if the liquid truly was 1% sulfuric acid, as the label on the jar indicated, it would not have caused the extent of the injuries I sustained.

Yet for me, doubts remained. It seemed a bit far-fetched to think that the old, blonde-haired woman and her ex-husband could have been involved in trafficking illegal drugs. I wanted to avoid jumping to conclusions. I voiced some of my misgivings to this family friend, and he recommended that I ask my chemistry teacher for his opinion.

I nodded in agreement. However, a few months passed by before I found the courage to ask my chemistry teacher about it. I was nervous to ask him because I wasn't sure I wanted to know the truth. What if the sulfuric acid had been used as an ingredient in the creation of drugs? I wasn't sure that the truth would make my life any easier.

After a few months of rumination, I crafted a plan to ask my chemistry teacher, Dr. Foster, for his opinion. One day, at the end of class, I remained seated while my classmates shuffled out of the room. I waited until everyone had left and then approached Dr. Foster.

Months before, at the beginning of the school year, I had introduced myself to Dr. Foster. I wanted him to know about the accident, in case any problems arose in class related to labs involving substances like sulfuric acid. I anticipated that the smells associated with these chemicals might bring back unpleasant memories for me and possibly create a triggering event. I was halfway through my introductory sentence with Dr. Foster when he interrupted me and said, "I know who you are."

Apparently, he knew about the accident.

"You're very blessed," he had said. "Things could have been much worse."

At the time, I was surprised that he knew about the accident. I assumed that my guidance counselor, Mr. Drake, must have told him about it.

As the school year unfolded, I witnessed Dr. Foster's passion for chemistry firsthand. During lessons, he would spit out facts, speaking excitedly about the pH scale, atoms, and chemical substances.

Sometimes I found Dr. Foster's confidence intimidating. His intellectual capabilities were evident not only in his scientific knowledge, but also in his choice of vocabulary. Despite my misgivings, I was determined to forge ahead on that spring day of my junior year. In light of our conversation at the beginning of the school year, I hoped this conversation with Dr. Foster would go well. Still, I was nervous.

"Dr. Foster," I said as I walked toward him. "Is it possible for sulfuric acid to be used in making drugs?"

The moment the words left my mouth, Dr. Foster stiffened. He looked down at something he was working on in the lab and said, "Yes, it could be possible." Yet he quickly shifted gears by saying that to create drugs, only a low concentration of acid was required.

To illustrate his point, he said that extracting acid out of a car battery would provide enough acid for the creation of illicit drugs. It was unlikely, he suggested, that anyone would need a jar filled with the substance to create drugs.

After a few more moments of explanation, a lull came over our conversation. I felt unsatisfied with his response. It seemed to me that Dr. Foster was saying that the sulfuric acid could not have been used for drugs because the concentration was too high.

Emboldened, I found a different way to ask the same question. I brought up how the woman had claimed that her ex-husband used the sulfuric acid for metal etching despite the fact that doctors had said the high concentration would have likely burned straight through the metal. "Was it not at all possible that they were using sulfuric acid as ingredients in drugs?" I asked.

Looking directly into my eyes, he said, "Anything is possible, but I think it is always good to try to see the best in people and take them at their word."

He seemed to be suggesting that I had no reason to question the woman's explanation. If she said the acid was for her ex-husband's metal etching, then it must be so.

Throughout our conversation, Dr. Foster appeared irritated, fidgeting and moving around his classroom. He seemed eager for our discussion to come to an end.

Soon after, I left the classroom. I walked down the hall trying to make sense of the conversation. I felt like I had failed to communicate my intentions. My goal had simply been to know the truth. I wasn't trying to impugn anyone's character or assume the worst of the people who had been in possession of the liquid substance. After all, I didn't even know the name of the woman's ex-husband.

Dr. Foster's reaction seemed strange. It felt like I had offended him. I was puzzled over why he would be offended by my question. Was he trying to defend something or someone? As I walked out of the classroom that day, I wondered what it was he could be hiding.

CHOOSING TO SEE

*To be blind is not miserable; not to be able
to bear blindness, that is miserable.*
—John Milton

"You know you could have been blind," Dr. Leo said with a hint of concern.

"Yeah," I said in response.

I was hardly surprised by Dr. Leo's assertion. After all, I had heard this before from numerous people, friends, and medical professionals.

"Do you think I would have committed suicide if I was blind?" I asked.

I had always wondered this but had never had the courage to voice the question. Uttering such a query forced me to examine the value I assigned to my own life. Was there a certain condition or set of circumstances that would hypothetically lead me to act upon such an impulse?

I did not have to wait long for Dr. Leo's response.

"No," he said as if he was sure.

"Why not?" I asked.

"Because you don't now, why would you then?" he said.

Despite his assurances, I still felt unsure. How could I know that I would not have taken more drastic measures if I had been blind? I wondered why this mattered so much to me. Sometimes, I felt as if I needed Dr. Leo to validate my experience or to confirm my self-worth.

As our session continued, I detected that this poignant part of our session was about to close. In my experience, counseling was filled with moments of great intensity followed by periods of relative calm. Eagerly, I took one last stab at retiring my persistent doubts for good.

"I guess the same reason I don't commit suicide now . . . I wouldn't have then," I said, repeating his already uttered words for good measure.

"Right," he said.

And with that, the issue was resolved. Dr. Leo had a way of doing that—summing up the most complicated questions or scenarios with just a few, simple words.

ROMANTIC BEGINNINGS

But love is blind, and lovers cannot see,
the pretty follies that themselves commit.
—Shakespeare, *The Merchant of Venice*

One morning during the spring of my junior year, I stood in a grocery store trying to decide which flowers to buy for my high school crush.

Red roses were too obvious. Yellow seemed too dull—or not obvious enough. White flowers seemed to strike the right balance, serving as a symbol of purity and beauty—a token of friendship with the possibility of something more. I decided to buy them.

Minutes later, I arrived at school with the flowers hidden in my backpack. I was shaking and felt like I could barely breathe. My plan kept running through my brain as I attempted to quiet my nerves. *What if she says no?* I wondered.

I sat next to Mary, the girl who had caught my fancy, at a table near the front of the classroom. The room was composed of large tables surrounded by green, metal chairs. This was the newspaper classroom, a class we had together. My love for writing had been nourished in this class, and I reassured myself while willing the butterflies in my stomach to subside. Then, one of our mutual friends decided to take matters into her own hands.

"I think you and Mary should go to prom!" Ellen exclaimed.

My heart stopped. Did she really just say that? I looked over at Mary. She and I exchanged an awkward smile. I shot Ellen a dirty look, hoping that she would refrain from saying anything else.

The beginning of my friendship with Mary dated back to freshman year. We developed a rapport during our newspaper and Latin classes, although our friendship deepened in the following years. Her kindness, compassion, and understanding drew me to her, and I began to feel something more for her. I liked her.

Suddenly, she put her pencil down on the table. As if on cue, I reached into my backpack, feeling around until the rose petals were resting against the palm of my hand.

"Oh hey, I read your article, and . . ." my voice trailed off as I pulled the most recent edition of our school newspaper out of my backpack and placed it on the table. Inside, I had found her article and typed out the following message:

Will you go to prom with me? Oh, by the way, nice article ☺.

After a second, I retrieved the flowers from my backpack and handed them to her.

As soon as she saw the flowers, she smiled. "Yes!" she said without hesitation, embracing me in a hug that I wished would last forever.

In a session with Dr. Leo, I told him about Mary.

"You know what they say, 'Being in love is the best medicine,'" Dr. Leo said. In the moment, I knew what he meant—not that I was in love with Mary, but that my excitement over liking someone had brightened my spirits. Smiling, he appeared happy for me, listening intently as I described my eagerness to venture into a new world of romance.

I was describing the tension I felt between Mary and myself, as if we both knew how the other felt but were afraid to vocalize our feelings.

"Should I ask her out?" I asked Dr. Leo.

He was cautious in his response but seemed mildly supportive. It was his job to be vague, I reminded myself. Occasionally, I wondered if he ever revealed his true thoughts.

"I want to end up with someone who knew me before the accident," I said.

"So they will understand?" He asked.

"Yeah," I said. I went on to explain how the boy I had been before the accident seemed so different from the man I was after it. No one would be able to truly understand me, I felt, unless they knew me before my life was altered.

He stopped for a moment, as if searching for the right response. "That desire will fade with time," he said. "You won't always feel that way."

I paused. I began to question my feelings for Mary. Did I actually like her, or did I just like that she knew me before the accident?

Either way, I was far from sure.

DAZED AND CONFUSED

I wish my brain had a map to tell me
where my heart should go . . .
—Unknown

Before Mary, the idea of pursuing a girl—or being liked by a girl—had eluded me. I had spent many of my adolescent years in and out of doctor's offices and medical facilities. It had not exactly been a time that fostered my attractiveness. I was coming to all of this a bit late and felt like I was behind my peers. I wasn't sure how prom would go, but I hoped that somehow I would be able to figure out whether Mary liked me or not.

On the day of prom, I picked her up for dinner. We were still in casual clothes, planning to change later that evening. I drove Mary to her friend's house where we all made dinner together, skipping the restaurant to save money. The group was a collection of Mary's friends, so I didn't know most of the people there. After dinner, the guys went downstairs to change into tuxedos while the girls went upstairs to get into their dresses.

After emerging from the basement, we waited for the ladies to descend the stairs. Families began to arrive, including my own, eager to snap pictures before the dance. Normally eager to avoid being photographed, I relaxed my policy for the night, excited to be photographed with Mary.

Eventually, the girls made their way to the top of the stairs. Seeing Mary in her dress took my breath away. I watched as she stood at the top of the stairs, walking toward me in a purple dress with a smile on her face. We met at the end of the stairs and my heart skipped a beat as we hugged.

Mary's father and I exchanged pleasantries while her mother was concerned for her daughter's safety. "I'm going to grill you," she said to me, much to Mary's chagrin. Her mother asked me several questions, including how I "liked to dance." Eventually, Mary pulled me away, rescuing me from the situation.

Soon after, we departed for the dance in a van driven by the parents of one of the students. In the car, Mary told me that her mom had pointed out to her that this was her "first date." Stunned, I waited to see what she would say next. "I guess it is," she said. I felt nervous as the van drove along, wondering what the dance would be like. We hardly spoke, exchanging only a few furtive glances throughout the drive.

Upon our arrival, Mary and I made our way into the ballroom. It was packed with students dancing. The room was dimly lit with tables set up in the far corners of the room. We sat for a few moments at one of the tables. It was too loud to talk, which worked in my favor because I didn't know what to say. After a few minutes of awkwardly sitting at the table, I asked her to dance.

We found a spot at the edge of the dance floor, and my heart began to race. As our hands met, fireworks erupted in my head. We danced for hours, refraining from conversation while instead exchanging smiles and laughter. As the night wore on, I began to wonder what she was thinking of me. *Did she like me? Was it possible that she could fall for me?*

In the middle of the night, with Bruno Mars crooning in the background, we looked into each other's eyes. I tried to figure out if she liked me. As she held my gaze, a smile broke out across her face.

My confidence began to swell. Perhaps someone like me could have a girlfriend after all.

Moments later, Ellen, the same friend who said that Mary and I should go to prom together, made her way toward us and pulled me to the side of the dance floor.

"So, is this going to go anywhere?" she asked.

"I don't know," I said.

I had not yet revealed my true feelings to Mary, and I wasn't exactly sure how to start that conversation on my own.

"Ok, I'll find out," she said as she disappeared with Mary.

A few moments later, Mary and Ellen appeared again. Ellen pulled me aside to offer a full report. The disappointed look on her face told me everything I needed to know.

"Sam, she just wants to be friends," she said apologetically.

"That's okay," I said. After all, I was hardly surprised.

How was anyone going to fall for me, scars and all?

A HERO'S CALLING

Courage is resistance to fear, mastery
of fear—not absence of fear.
—Mark Twain

Near the end of my junior year, my class held a career day. This meant that students could shadow a professional for the day in any field of work. Throughout the year, I had been pondering a career as a mental health professional. I thought that if I went into the field of psychology, I could draw upon my own experiences and trauma to help someone else. It felt like a meaningful way to make sense of my own painful experience.

With that in mind, I arranged to shadow a counselor. On the appointed day, I drove in my car, searching for a building farther off the highway than I expected. I eventually found it, tucked behind a group of trees. I walked inside and met Mr. Edwards. He was slightly overweight and wore glasses and a goatee. He specialized in working with troubled youth.

I don't remember much from the day except for something Mr. Edwards said. When he described his approach to counseling, he said that his job was not to directly solve problems for his clients.

"We want them to be the heroes in their own stories," he said with a smile.

Weeks later, I talked about this experience with Dr. Leo.

"Do you want me to be the hero in my story?" I asked him.

"Yes . . . and you are," he said.

A FATHER'S LOVE

*Hear, O sons, a father's instruction, and be
attentive, that you may gain insight.*
—Proverbs 4:1

One evening that summer, my family and I had dinner with Michael and Miriam, the friends who had visited me the day of the accident in the hospital. Memories came flooding back as I saw them again for the first time in years.

"Sam, take your glasses off. Let me look at you," Michael said.

His words made me feel a bit like a museum piece, but I complied with his request. I removed my glasses and he stared at me intently, moving his face forward until it was just a few inches from mine.

"Well, you look great!" he declared, almost like he was surprised.

I didn't know how to respond.

"When have I not looked great?" I said, half-jokingly.

"Well . . ." he hesitated.

"Yes, there was a time when I didn't look so great," I conceded. "I was recently looking at pictures from the day after the accident, and it is like night and day between then and now. And that is what you saw," I told him. "And I still remember the look on your face in the hospital. You were really holding it in," I told him sincerely.

Taken aback, I could see a flash of emotion cross his face, mixed with surprise.

"Yeah, it was tough," he said. "We didn't know if you would survive."

On the car ride home, I asked my father some questions. I had wanted to ask him about the accident from his perspective for years, but never had. For the most part, my father kept his feelings to himself. I had heard second-hand about tears he had shed while at a back-to-school night held days after the accident. Apparently, my father had been standing with my younger siblings when someone asked him how I was doing. In response, my father had sobbed. This story did little to mollify my desire to learn more about my father's feelings.

"Did you know if I would survive?" I asked my father.

"No," he said.

"Are you glad I survived?" I asked.

"I am very glad," he said. "I wouldn't have it any other way. If you hadn't survived, I never would have gotten over it."

And while my father had said he loved me countless times before, this was the first time since the accident that I truly felt the depth of his love.

———

Samuel Moore-Sobel

It was nearly a year after that conversation with my father when a neighbor startled me with an unexpected tidbit about him.

"Your dad used to take long runs, you know," she said. Meaning, after the accident.

She continued, saying that she used to see him run for long distances after my injuries. "He looked reflective," she said, as if he had been trying to work through what happened to his son.

I tried to picture the scene in my mind but had a hard time picturing a look of tender emotion on my father's face.

As an ex-policeman and distance runner, my father had always been the very definition of strength. His muscles and defined biceps were especially striking to me as a young boy. He could move anything and carry everything. No task was too hard for him. When he was managing a landscaping company, he could dig a hole faster than the men who worked for him. Physically, he was everything I aspired to be.

I had watched him run countless times before. When he ran, he balanced his physical strength with grace. I could see him pumping his arms and legs while running through the streets, his eyes trained a few steps ahead and a look of determination on his face.

As the conversation with my neighbor ended, I went back into the house. *I wish I could have seen those runs*, I thought to myself. Perhaps then I would have better understood my father.

A BEARDED EXPERIMENT

And here I sat a long, long time, waiting
patiently for the world to know me . . .
—Nathaniel Hawthorne

Since only days after the accident, I was obsessed with the idea of growing a beard. "Soldiers returning from the Civil War grew beards," a family member told me once, suggesting that a beard was a better alternative to plastic surgery. Others echoed his sentiment in the weeks following the accident. Facial hair, I gathered from a chorus of voices, was an excellent way to hide my scars from the world.

This desire ignored the fact that my ability to grow a beard was hampered by my scars. For instance, my mustache grew in with an empty space in the middle of it. The hair surrounding my chin refused to grow in correctly, making it look as if there was a hole in the center of my beard.

Reaching senior year brought a welcome change. The surgery

performed by Dr. Michaels had reduced the size of the scar in the middle of my upper lip, allowing hair to grow without a noticeable gap. The work done on my chin also reduced the hole in the center of my beard. After the surgery, I let my hair grow out. My facial hair grew, coming in wispy on the sides while thick around my chin and neck. People responded positively to my new look, leading me to believe that I finally had an adequate way to improve my appearance. Much to my surprise, I felt a new sense of confidence whenever I caught a glimpse of myself in the mirror.

My father was thrilled by my facial hair. Upon seeing my beard, he said triumphantly, "It's about time!" His reaction encapsulated how I felt. I was free from the need to explain my scars and no longer had to look at them myself. Finally, I could simply be me.

While everyone seemed to offer encouragement about my change in appearance, my mother was noticeably quiet. Sometimes what she chose not to say was more telling than what she did say. After a few weeks, I finally summoned the courage to ask for her opinion. "Do you like it?" I asked.

She looked away. After a few seconds, she turned her head back toward me and said, "I like you best clean-shaven," she said, before identifying the main reason I hadn't shaved. "You're using the beard to hide," she said quietly.

HELPING ME SEE

The question is not what you look at, but what you see.
—Henry David Thoreau

Late in my junior year, I took a job in the children's center of a local gym. My job was to supervise children while their parents exercised, playing games and sports with the kids.

It was there that I met Helen, a colleague at the gym and a mother of two. Helen had short brown hair, a contagious laugh, and an infectious smile. Her energy brightened the room. Her clear, blue eyes held a depth that I had rarely seen before.

I didn't notice her scars until a few weeks after we met. She had long, deep marks running down the inside of her arms. Oddly enough, they looked a bit like my scars. It looked as if hers had faded a bit, and the marks could easily be confused for veins. They looked as if someone in a fit of rage had taken a knife and carved into her skin.

One day in the middle of a conversation, she happened to reveal her story. She had been diagnosed with cancer as a young adult and wasn't sure if she would survive. As a result, she underwent years of treatment. Chemotherapy took a toll on her body, forcing her to face immense pain and increasing uncertainty.

She survived the cancer, but evidence of it remained in both apparent and hidden ways. Most notably, the cancer stole her ability to give birth. Instead, she and her husband decided to adopt. As she shared this part of the story, she looked at her daughters playing nearby.

As she neared the end of her story, she leaned toward me. We were separated by a shelf filled with children's shoes, so she draped her arm over the shelf while gently pointing to her scars.

I was shocked by her willingness to share this intimate part of her experience. The irony was not lost on me. I had spent the past few years attempting to hide my scars, while she willingly shared hers with me.

To her, the marks were evidence of her survival. She seemed proud of them—not because they reminded her of pain, but because they reminded her of life.

After a few moments, her arms returned to her side. She smiled, and only then did I wonder if she knew more than she let on about the scars on my face.

I thanked her for showing me her scars, appreciative of the hope she had given me. In response, I shared my story with her and pointed out the scars on my face.

"Oh, but Sam, you look wonderful," she said in response. "I am so glad you are here."

A few weeks after our conversation, she submitted her resignation. She had kept the job simply for the perk of a free gym membership but decided it was time to pursue a new endeavor. I was sad to see her go, thanking her once again for letting me see her scars. She hugged me, pulling me into a warm embrace. "Life is a gift," she said. "A wonderful gift."

After talking to Helen, I found new inspiration to view my life and circumstances differently. Unlike Helen, I was not actively treasuring every second of my life. It was too easy to forget that my life could have ended when I was fifteen years old. I decided to reflect on the ways in which I had grown since the accident. I wanted to savor life, not rush through it. Cheating death could offer me a new perspective, if I chose to embrace it. I was free to enjoy the beauty of the world—the clouds on the horizon and the trees in the distance—all while taking a deep breath and offering a heartfelt thanks for the life I had before, for the life I had now, and for the life still to come.

ANOTHER CELEBRATION OF LIFE

This is the day that the Lord has made;
let us rejoice and be glad in it.
—Psalm 118:24

The second anniversary of the accident snuck up on me more than it had the previous year. As the end of July rolled around, I felt a surge of emotion. I found myself routinely upset by the most insignificant occurrences—running into traffic, a class running late, or my homework not being exactly as I anticipated. I was keenly aware of situations in which I did not have full control and felt a heightened sense of angst whenever things did not go according to plan.

Once August was underway, I suddenly realized why this was happening: the anniversary of the accident was just weeks away. This would occur again, in later years. It was like my body felt the milestone coming more than my mind did. It automatically went into high alert, usually beginning around the last week of July and throughout all of August, as if in preparation for what was to come.

In anticipation of the second anniversary of the accident, I did my best to gear up for the overwhelming emotions those few weeks would likely bring. Despite the resolution my family and I had made the year before to commemorate the day with a celebration, I struggled to stay true to this plan. I felt tempted to despair over all that had been lost instead of celebrating all that I had.

Near the end of August, I was walking to school when I ran into my friend Parker. "You know, it is just like any other day," he said, as I shared with him about my apprehension concerning the upcoming anniversary. "And it's a brand new month. A fresh start. In my family, we wake up on the first day of every month and say to each other, 'Rabbit, rabbit,' for good luck."

That's strange, I thought. But it left me thinking. I was eager to try new things to make September 1 a celebratory day, so I decided to incorporate this phrase into my vocabulary. I didn't believe in luck, but it felt like a cheerful, positive way to confront the milestone. And it worked for Parker, so maybe it would work for me.

———

My first class on August 31 was PEER, again taught by Mrs. Allen. Since PEER was a two-year program for the students selected during their junior year, I started my senior year in a comfortable environment. Since our first day of class fell on the day before the anniversary of the accident, she suggested that I share my story with the group.

I could see the benefit of sharing my story so early in the academic year. It could help me clear the air with my classmates and maybe avoid any unwanted questions about my scars. On the other hand, I worried about how my peers would respond. I didn't want to overwhelm them with the heaviness of my story, especially the classmates I had never met before. I also wasn't sure I wanted this to be their very first impression of me.

In the end, at Mrs. Allen's convincing, I decided to share my story.

Her classroom was organized with a large circle of desks around the middle of the room. The classroom had white walls and little light. On that day in August, I sat in the middle of the room in a rolling chair with my classmates sitting in desks around me. Mrs. Allen began the class by asking me a few questions, warming me up before I started the story.

Then it was time, and I began. "Almost two years ago, I was hired for a day to move boxes and furniture . . ." My heart began to ache as I continued, and feelings of grief welled up inside me as I looked around at the room full of shocked faces. My voice got shaky, but I pressed on.

"Then, I saw some sort of liquid substance flying towards my face," I said. I tried to describe the pain, but felt unable to fully encapsulate what it felt like to burn alive, just as I always do when recounting my experience. When I finished speaking, the room was silent. I looked around at my classmates in the circle and wondered if I had shared too much. After what felt like an eternity, a fellow classmate piped up.

"Well, you look great," she said.

Mrs. Allen chimed in, her words aimed not just toward me, but all of her students.

"You think everyone notices the imperfections we possess," she said. "The pimples, disfigurements, and the scars that each one of us carries. We think everyone must know since they play so prominently in our own minds. Our fixation upon our imperfections are rarely shared by anyone outside of our own heads. Just remember that you notice it more than anyone else," she said.

Perhaps it was true that others did not notice my scars in the same way that I did. I knew my scars more intimately than anyone else—and each of my scar's peculiarities: how they grew more or less noticeable depending on the weather, or how they felt better on cold days than on hot days. How they became a certain pink color in cold weather, rather than a deep red as in the summer months. There were things about my scars that only I knew because I carried them with me each and every day. They were a part of me and always would be.

But I couldn't quite accept Mrs. Allen's statement that no one noticed my scars. To the contrary, I frequently received questions about my face, especially upon meeting someone for the first time.

Mrs. Allen's words softened the students and my classmates began sharing their thoughts more freely.

"It controlled you. Now you control it," my friend Chase said to me.

"I tip my hat to you every day," my friend Amber said.

Another added, "You've grown so much. What happened to you shouldn't have happened, I agree with you, but what you have done with it is you have turned it into an opportunity."

Suddenly, more classmates jumped in to offer words and sentiments. It was as if a dam had burst.

"You just seem so strong, and your story affects me. It affects all of us," one classmate said.

"Your story encourages others to live out your example," said another.

In many ways, I felt incredibly undeserving of such sentiments. I thought about all of the days when I had acted like a child, sulking in the corner over all that I had lost. As I continued listening to my classmates' responses, I felt like a fraud.

"I want you here," Mrs. Allen said to me. "I think the world of you, and I'll do anything for you, so you can come and find me tomorrow."

I could see the sincerity in her eyes.

"Tonight, think about the perfect day," she said. "You had this experience happen to you that changed your life, but it doesn't define you."

Later that night, I took her suggestion to heart and did my best to envision my perfect day. I imagined myself in the middle of an open field, with unobstructed plains as far as I could see. As I ran through the field, my family came into view. They were sitting on the ground, looking content. The sun blazed down upon us and I felt its warmth.

In the middle of my dreaming, I paused. I tried to picture how my face would look. Despite my best efforts, nothing came to mind. I couldn't think of any version of my face without scars—I could only see a blank face, like clay waiting to be shaped.

I longed to experience one more day before the accident. I would use it to hug my parents, brother, and sister. I would tell them how much I loved them and how much they meant to me. I would run through the field from my imagination and soak in the sun's rays. I'd savor that moment as if it were my last.

On September 1, 2011, the second anniversary of the accident, the world seemed to travel in slow motion. I couldn't focus at school on anything other than memories of the past. My body was present, but my mind was far away.

The day progressed just as any other. I attended classes and greeted friends in the hallway. I walked from class to class wondering if anyone else detected my distress. I wanted to remain in control of my emotions and tried my best to act normally.

For most of the day, I did this successfully. That is, until Latin class. It was my last class of the day, and victory was within reach. I daydreamed about running out of the classroom door. I longed to sprint through the halls, past the double white doors, out into the parking lot. I wanted to go home, see my family, and enjoy a quiet dinner. I wanted to marvel at the journey of the last two years. *Just one more class*, I reminded myself.

The class started, but I still couldn't focus. The afternoon dragged on, and I kept looking at the clock. I watched as the seconds ticked by, and the hands neared three o'clock. Right then, my mind returned to the day of the accident. I started replaying the details of the day over and over again. As memories came flooding back, my hands began to shake, and my breathing slowed. No matter how hard I tried, I couldn't stop thinking about the accident.

I reminded myself that the accident was in the past. I took a deep breath and exhaled slowly. I tried to distract myself by listening to the lesson. Despite my efforts, my glances at the clock increased as the little hand passed the six.

The class ended at 3:48, which nearly coincided with the time that the acid had hit my face two years before. My right leg began to shake. I waited for the bell to ring and release me from that prison.

In that moment, two classmates unexpectedly approached with pieces of paper in their hands. They handed me the papers and returned to their seats. They were also in PEER, and I wondered if this gesture had been prompted by the story I had shared the day before. Moments later, the bell rang, and we filed out of the classroom one by one. I held the papers in my hand as I walked through the hallway. To my surprise, a handful of students who had heard my story in PEER the day before gathered around me, hugging me and whispering words of support.

After a few moments, we dispersed. I walked toward the exit of the school, rummaging my way through hordes of students. I reached for the papers from my classmates. I was surprised by what greeted me:

"Sam," one of the letters began.

First, I want to start out by saying what an inspiration you are. You are the kindest, most compassionate guy I know. I have truly been blessed that our paths have crossed this past year, and I'm really excited to get to know you on a more personal level this year through PEER. Just hearing you talk yesterday in PEER really touched my heart. I know how hard it can be to find light in times of darkness, so hearing about how much you've overcome and how you've dealt with this whole situation has really opened my eyes. I just want you to know that you are making a difference and touching the lives of many people. You are strong and courageous, and it takes a very special person to get through this. I have faith that one day you will forget about all of the bad things associated with this situation and that there will only be positive thoughts on how you've changed as a stronger person and how you've changed others. You're an amazing role model to any age. Just keep in mind that you have many people behind you who have your back, especially today (and everyday :)). I know this was kind of random, but I just felt like I needed to tell you what a great inspiration you are to me. I'll be thinking of you and praying for you as the day continues so that you will eventually be able to REDEFINE the day.

Stay strong :)
Your friend,
Christine

I felt a wave of emotion as I read her words. Christine and I didn't know each other well—and even though she struck me as a kind and caring person, I could never have anticipated the gift of her beautiful words. My concerns about whether or not my story from the day before in PEER had scared my fellow classmates quickly faded. Perhaps Mrs. Allen was right to have me speak about my experience after all. I traveled home that day feeling thankful for Christine's words and empowered to take on whatever came next.

JUDGING A BOOK BY ITS COVER

Beauty is in the eye of the beholder.
—Unknown

"The first thing people notice about me is my scars," I told my friend Chase.

"We all notice physical appearance, Sam. Everyone does," he said in response. He went on to say that we all make snap judgments about the essence of a person based on our perception of their physical appearance. Upon meeting someone for the first time, people can be drawn to certain characteristics. Everyone assigns terms, based on what they see: fat, skinny, ugly, handsome, beautiful.

I had never thought about first impressions in these terms.

Chase and I continually engaged in conversations such as these over the remainder of our high school years, attempting to make our way towards adulthood. I felt liberated at times to be vulnerable with

Chase, to admit feelings that I otherwise took great pains to conceal throughout my interactions with nearly everyone else—even topics that I found embarrassing to talk about, such as my non-existent social life. Throughout my high school years, I felt like I was missing out on so much. While my friends were out playing high school sports, I was prepping for surgery. While most others in our high school class were going to parties and having fun, I was recovering from a recent operation. While I felt as if nearly everyone was in a romantic relationship, or at least going on dates, I was left wondering whether or not anyone would ever want to go out with me because of all that I had been through.

This all came to a head on my eighteenth birthday. At my parents urging, I excitedly organized a party to celebrate. In true twenty-first century fashion, I sent out invitations on Facebook and brimmed with anticipation at the thought of celebrating my birthday with a group of friends. On the appointed day, much to my disappointment, only a handful of friends showed up. I was devastated, and as the night wore on, I felt the sting of rejection and loneliness more and more.

Chase had been one of the few to attend my party, and after the others left, we talked late into the night. I was frustrated and started doing what I nearly always did: blaming myself. *Perhaps I didn't talk about the party enough,* I thought, failing to do enough work to enlist my friends to attend. As our conversation unfolded, I asked Chase how he thought our fellow classmates perceived me. I had long struggled with that notion, wondering what my peers thought of me after my life had been turned upside down. Perhaps I was doing something to keep people at arm's length, to dissuade them from choosing to be closer friends with me.

"I think they think you know," he said.

"Know what?" I asked, trying to understand what he meant.

He answered quietly, "You walk down the hall as if you know things that no one else knows."

I did not know what he meant. What did I possibly know that everyone else didn't? I felt quite the opposite, as if everyone else knew more than I did.

As we continued talking, Chase revealed his own struggles. I had always assumed that he was wildly popular—he was at the top of our class, competing for the top spot of valedictorian with just a few others. He was president of our class, he exuded charisma, and he was well-respected throughout the student body. Yet that night, he revealed that he, too, had what he considered to be a lack of a social life. So much of his time was spent focused on school and extracurricular activities, so much so that he felt as if he didn't have room for anything else. He also said that despite his apparent popularity, there were a lot of Friday and Saturday nights that he spent at home. He seemed surprised by his lack of invitations to parties and social engagements and was left to ponder many of the same thoughts with which I was grappling.

Oddly enough, his words made me feel a bit better. If Chase had trouble in this area, I figured it wasn't so out of the ordinary that I would, too. He left as night began to turn into early morning, vowing that we would spend more time together socially in the near future.

Months later, Chase fully explained what he meant when he told me that he thought my life was better than his.

"Would you like to trade with me?" I said. "Would you like to wake up in the mirror and see what I see?"

Without missing a beat, Chase fired back, "Yes, because when you look in the mirror, you don't ask the question, 'Who am I?'"

I was stunned. How could Chase want to be me?

HELLO AND GOODBYE, DEAR WILLIAMSBURG

We live as we dream—alone.
—Joseph Conrad, *Heart of Darkness*

During my last summer as a high school student, I attended a pre-collegiate program at the College of William & Mary. It was a magical summer filled with opportunities to learn more about one of my favorite subjects—American history. I fell in love with the college the moment I stepped foot onto the beautiful grounds. The campus, steeped in colonial history, boasted an impressive list of alumni, including three past American presidents. I could sense the air of prestige as I walked through the halls, as if the caliber of both students and professors was tangible. After experiencing this place that encouraged intellectual jousting, cultivated dry wit, and fostered vibrant conversation, I determined that it was the institution of higher education for me.

Through this experience, I made lifelong friends. A few of us decided to apply to the college. My friend Griffin and I even decided to be roommates, planning out our lives after high school.

Even though it had only been three weeks, Griffin and I became fast friends from the beginning. I'll never forget the first night we met. A few hours after our arrival at the program, the resident assistants led an icebreaker, using a Sharpie to write questions on a beach ball. We stood in a large semicircle passing the ball around. Whenever someone caught the ball, they had to answer one of the questions written on it.

When Griffin caught the ball, he looked down at the question his hands landed on. "Would you rather visit London or Paris?" he said in a southern drawl. "Well, I guess London . . . because they speak English there," he said.

The room erupted in laughter, struck by the innocence and sincerity with which he spoke.

As the three-week program came to an end, one of the professors agreed to write a recommendation letter to accompany my admissions application. The professor was an older man who had spent decades cultivating his reputation within his field. I was excited that he would write such a letter on my behalf and felt like it was a sure sign I would gain admission to the college.

As I prepared my application materials, an admissions officer from the college came to visit my high school. I sat wide-eyed during his presentation, listening for insight about how to achieve my dream of attending the college.

Afterward, I approached the admissions officer to see what information I could gather. I knew that while my grade point average was good, it was far from spectacular. There would be hundreds, if not thousands, of students applying with much more impressive academic credentials, but I figured my compelling life story provided a unique advantage. After all, how many other students applying knew through experience what it was like to be burned with sulfuric acid?

I shared the story of the accident with the admissions officer and asked if he thought my story would be an influential factor in the admissions process.

"All applications are thoroughly reviewed," he said. He mentioned the importance of grades and SAT scores and appeared unaffected by my story.

I found his words to be extremely discouraging. I walked back to my classroom, wondering if my dreams would inevitably be dashed when I submitted my application.

Part of the challenge was that I believed my story was enough to gain acceptance into nearly any college I wanted. This had been reinforced by several people in my life. For example, my principal, an alum of William & Mary, agreed to write a recommendation letter on my behalf. "You definitely have a good shot," he told me. My guidance counselor repeatedly reassured me that my chances of acceptance were high. Other teachers seconded these statements.

After what felt like an eternity, I received word from William & Mary. I jumped out of my bed the moment I saw the email pop into my inbox.

I opened it excitedly and read the first sentence.

"We regret to inform you . . ." it said.

I stared at the screen in disbelief. I felt numb. Just weeks before, I had been accepted into Drexel University, but it wasn't the college I wanted to attend. I had applied to nine schools, but there was only one I wanted to attend—and it had just rejected me.

Devastated, I called my friend Griffin. As soon as I heard his voice, he asked me if I had been accepted. I told him about my rejection, and he sounded surprised.

"I cannot believe you didn't get in," he said. "You should have gotten in."

Soon after, he read me the email he had received, informing him of his waitlisted status. He declared in a fit of rage that even if they offered him admission, he would decline.

"At least you got waitlisted," I told him.

Before he could respond, our call was disconnected. He tried to call me back, only to be disconnected seconds after the connection was made. This cycle continued for several minutes.

I paced back and forth in the basement as I repeatedly called him back, our attempts to reconnect thwarted by forces far outside of our control. When we finally connected, he delivered an expletive-laden rebuke of the events surrounding the day. "And after all you have been through," he said with a drop in his voice.

His empathy and compassion came through the phone helping to restore my sense of self in a moment where my confidence was low. Little did I know that this sentiment would be repeated by many in the days and weeks ahead. Somehow other people in my life seemed to understand the stakes involved as I navigated the college admissions process. Inevitably, rejection struck a deeper chord for me than it would have otherwise because I had already lost so much through the accident.

As my call with Griffin ended, I trekked up the stairs to the kitchen. Sitting down at the table in the center of the room, I stared at my laptop. My mother, brother, and father entered the kitchen making feeble attempts to cheer me up. I vented, hoping that the more words I spoke, the more this would all finally make sense. I was physically present, but my mind was far away bidding adieu to a place I had hoped to one day call home.

CLOAKED IN ANGER

Anger is an acid that can do more harm to the vessel in which it is stored than to anything on which it is poured.
—Mark Twain

By the spring of my senior year, I was upset by the mounting rejection letters I had received from colleges. One day, as I sat in the library with my friend Amber, I decided to share my frustrations. She was a fellow PEER student, and I knew that she would be empathetic.

I told her how I felt defeated. I tried to console myself to no avail. She listened to my sad tale before interjecting with her thoughts.

"You have been complacent in your anger," she said.

Her words caught me off guard and forced me to wrestle with the depth of my feelings. While it appeared that I was angry at everything and everyone, the truth was a bit more complicated. Much of my anger was directed at myself. For not being smarter or stronger. For failing to live up to the high expectations I had placed on myself. For failing to achieve my full potential. For failing to be the person I thought I was meant to be.

"None of this is fair," I said. "And no one cares."

"People do care, Sam," Amber replied.

With a look of sincerity, she tried to offer perspective.

"I am not as strong as you are," she said. If the accident had happened to her, she said, "I could not have come to school with a smile on my face every day."

"You have every right to be angry," she said before advising me to continue working through my feelings. "Also," she said, "you are using the beard to cloak your anger."

Her words cut to my core. Reminiscent of my mother's words pointing out that I was using my beard to "hide," I recognized the truth. The beard was helping me hide—and to pretend like nothing had happened to my face. Tricking myself or others into accepting this alternate reality did not mollify my emotions. Amber's words were an important reminder that I was trying to mask reality. Even with a beard, I was still in pain.

CAPTIVATE WITH THE EYES

Eyes are the windows to the soul.
—William Shakespeare

Just weeks before high school graduation, I was invited to dinner at the home of Randy and Abigail.

I had met them during my freshman year of high school at a Bible study. After the accident, I attended only a handful of meetings. Randy and Abigail led the group and had done their best to keep in touch with me. They hosted a dinner for the graduating seniors and invited me back as an honorary member.

Abigail had a way about her as if she had information that no one else did. Her eyes were penetrating, with the ability to cut right to a person's soul. Everyone was drawn to her, and she spoke with understanding and compassion.

Throughout dinner, the table conversation was lively. Some asked me questions, eager to catch up on all that had occurred in the inter-vening years. I chatted away, filling everyone in on my adventures. Eventually, the group dissipated until I was the only one left with Abigail and Randy.

"Would you like to come sit down?" Abigail asked, inviting me to sit on the couch.

She proceeded to ask me questions about my life after the accident. I answered and then asked if they had noticed my scars when they first saw me earlier that evening.

"The first thing I noticed were your eyes," Abigail said.

"My eyes? What about them?" I asked.

"The depth, the maturity, the age," she replied.

You have eyes like that, too, I thought.

Abigail then told me about her previous, abusive marriage.

"I used to go and sit in the cemetery because I felt as dead as the people in those graves," she said.

After much pain, Abigail escaped her former husband and forged a new life. In the process, she met Randy—a man full of kindness, gentleness, and humor. Theirs was a story of love and redemption.

Abigail and I connected over the similarities of our journeys toward healing. I talked about the physical and emotional pain that I was still experiencing along with the distance I felt from God. I felt empty, half-convinced that what happened to me was the result of my own actions, while the other half of me knew there was nothing I could have done to sidestep that box of sulfuric acid.

"Do you think I will always feel this way?" I asked.

"The good parts will start filling the empty parts," Abigail said. "The good overcomes the bad. God has a plan."

I wish I knew the plan, I thought to myself.

"And when you find someone who accepts you for who you are, scars and all . . ." she said.

With tears streaming down my face, I shuddered, having convinced myself long before that no one would ever fall in love with me.

Her words were reminiscent of a recent session with Dr. Leo.

"Until you meet the right person . . ." he had said, referring to meeting the person I would marry. If I continued working toward healing, he reasoned, I could reach the "one-yard line." But he suggested that, for me, a place of healing might also involve finding someone who would fully love and accept me, scars and all.

Others had echoed these sentiments, leading me to believe that healing would remain just out of reach until I fell in love with the girl of my dreams. I knew these were well-meaning statements, but I found the words discouraging and worried that my physical appearance and emotional baggage meant that I wouldn't be able to find someone to love me. It felt like this last piece of healing was, and always would be, just out of reach.

GRADUATION DAY

Everything has to come to an end, sometime.
—L. Frank Baum, *The Marvelous Land of Oz*

My last session with Dr. Leo felt like a momentous occasion. In some ways, it felt even more important than my graduation from high school. I had grown immensely since my first session with Dr. Leo. We both knew that this day was coming. After all, my need for therapy had decreased. I found myself navigating situations more and more on my own. With Dr. Leo's help, I had spent the last two and a half years developing an arsenal of emotional tools. After years of struggling, I was finally ready for the next chapter.

Dr. Leo sat in his chair while I lounged in my usual spot on the couch. I had a habit of arranging the pillows under each of my arms, serving as a support when things went awry. I could grab on to them and use them as a stabilizing force when the therapy session became difficult or emotions started to rise.

I knew there was wisdom in moving on and ending therapy, but saying goodbye to Dr. Leo still felt hard.

We talked a bit about my upcoming transition to college. I had agonized over my decision of where to attend. My father wanted me to attend George Mason University, a school within driving distance of my parents' home. Yet others were recommending a different course, including Dr. Leo.

"It will be good for you to go away," he had said. His words echoed what nearly everyone other than my father told me. I, too, believed that traveling to a new home would be healing for me: to live in a place where no one knew about the accident. I decided to attend Drexel University in Philadelphia, Pennsylvania.

"Are you nervous?" Dr. Leo asked.

"A little," I told him, mixed with excitement. After all, Drexel was not my first choice, but I believed that it was far enough away from home for me to build a new life. Despite my remaining disappointment over being rejected from the College of William & Mary, I resolved that Drexel would do.

I felt prepared to attend college, so I shifted gears, choosing to focus my last session with Dr. Leo on my feelings of guilt. I felt guilty for allowing the accident to occur and for the effect it had on my family.

"How do I lessen my feelings of guilt?" I asked him.

"The accident wasn't your fault," Dr. Leo said. He had often repeated this refrain; however, his words didn't make me feel less guilty. I felt like I was carrying a heavy weight, aching for relief but unable to find it.

Dr. Leo went on to encourage me to think logically. He urged me to combat irrational thoughts with logical statements. It was an empowering message in theory, but in practice, sometimes my emotions trumped logic.

I began asking Dr. Leo questions.

"If you could take the acid for any of your kids, would you do it?" I asked.

"Yes, absolutely. Any parent would or should," he said.

"Right," I answered. "So why didn't God, as the loving Father, take it for me?"

Dr. Leo was silent for a few moments. "Well, that's the mystery," he said. "We'll never know. But I will say that only God has the ability to take something tragic and make something good out of it. He watched His Son die on the cross, yet through that, He provided salvation for the world."

I was looking forward to embarking on my college career. It felt like a perfect opportunity to turn over a new leaf. I told Dr. Leo what my mother had said a few days before: "I think you just have to move on," she had said. "Isn't that we are all doing right now—just moving on?"

My mother did not fixate on the past. She raised us to learn from the past, appropriately grieve losses when they arise, and carry on toward the next adventure. After nearly three years of wrestling with the accident, I felt ready for whatever came next.

I felt nostalgic as my last session with Dr. Leo came to an end. As he led me out of the office one last time, I turned around to take it all in. We had done good work here, he and I. I had grown through our sessions and felt that I had achieved some healing. I knew that I would miss him—even if I didn't know exactly how to tell him that I would.

As I made my way towards the car, he lingered, grasping for a few more moments of conversation. He stood tall on the sidewalk, but his eyes looked contemplative. It was as if he knew that, despite his confidence in me, we could not predict the future—and no matter how ready I was, he would no longer be there to help me.

I reassured him that I would be okay. "I might see a counselor at school," I said.

"Well, see how you feel. I am sure you will be fine," Dr. Leo said. "Let me know how everything turns out."

FACING THE FUTURE

Fear urged him to go back, but growth drove him on.
—Jack London, *White Fang*

Pain and scars. This was the topic of a seminar I found myself in just months after high school graduation. The seminar was led by author and businessman Jim Maxim. He had written a story in his book about a car accident that left him with severe facial scarring. Afterward, I went up to talk to him.

"I can really relate to your story," I said. Motioning toward my face, I pointed out the scars.

"Oh, is that what this is?" he responded, pointing to the areas on his own face, as if trying to mirror the images he saw in front of him.

"Yes," I said.

"Well, you look great!" he said.

"If you are comfortable answering, how long did it take for you to look like you do today?" I asked reticently, feeling guilty the moment the question left my lips.

"Well, this is forty years later," Maxim told me.

"Yeah, but how long did it take you to look like you do now?" I pressed on, eager to attach a timetable to a recovery that often felt unpredictable.

He cocked his head to the side with a thoughtful look on his face, calling old memories to mind.

"I guess about ten years," he said.

He looked down as he said it, then slowly brought his head back up until his gaze met mine. He looked pained.

Suddenly it hit me. Even forty years after the accident, I might have that same look of pain.

CATCHING MY BREATH

Given the choice between the experience of
pain and nothing, I would choose pain.
—William Faulkner, *The Wild Palms [If I Forget Thee, Jerusalem]*

I felt confused as I teetered on the edge of a panic attack. Everything turned blurry in an instant.

My chest heaved back and forth, and I made feeble attempts to get oxygen into my lungs. None came. My efforts made things worse, sending me into a state of paralysis.

I began to hyperventilate, unable to control the pace of my breathing. My pulse quickened, and my heart started racing. I felt weak in my knees, unable to stand upright. I leaned against my bed with my arms outstretched. I could not control my racing thoughts. I wiped sweat off my brow. Fear shot through my body. I felt like I was having a heart attack.

This wasn't supposed to happen, I thought to myself.

I had assumed when I traveled one hundred seventy miles north to attend Drexel University that the past would not follow me. I had believed Dr. Leo and the chorus of other voices that predicted a change in scenery was exactly what I needed. Yet here I was, having a panic attack in my dorm room, even though there were no tangible reminders of the accident.

Finally, my symptoms subsided and I wondered what to do next. I wanted to prevent this from happening again, so I decided to contact Dr. Leo. This panic attack felt like a regression in my health, and I wanted to do all I could to avoid experiencing a future panic attack.

I called Dr. Leo and told him what happened. He was calm and collected. It was strange talking to him over the phone. I thought we would never speak again after our last session. It was good to hear his voice again.

He reassured me that my experience was not abnormal, noting that patients could experience panic attacks with little warning, even years after a traumatic event. He recommended that I take Ativan on an as-needed basis. He thought that having a prescription on hand would be enough to prevent future panic attacks since my mind would be eased by the presence of a remedy.

"The more you dwell on this, the more you make it a problem," he said. "Go back to the toolbox," he said, "and if you run out of other tools, turn to medicine as a last resort."

I was slightly comforted, but still felt worried. I told him that another prescription felt like a step backward.

"This isn't a step backward," Dr. Leo said, "but simply something that happens."

"I've been doing a lot of writing," I told him. In an effort to capture all of the details of my story before my memories faded, I had been intentionally dedicating blocks of time to write it all down.

"That's good," he said. "Writing can also dredge up emotions from the past. But keep writing," he said quietly.

His words surprised me. I hadn't thought about how writing could cause distress.

After our conversation ended, I called my parents. I told them about my conversation with Dr. Leo. Surprisingly, my father responded by offering to pick up my prescription. He had always been at his best when he felt he could do something to help: run an errand, make a call. If I gave him a job, he was more than willing to help. He said he supported the idea of medication, just in case another panic attack occurred.

My father, once strongly opposed to medication, had unexpectedly offered his support.

Weeks later, I visited home. I walked in the door and my father handed me the bottle of Ativan as if he was proud of the decision I had made to manage my health. I reveled in the moment, grateful to connect with my father.

"Focus on something other than yourself," he told me, "and you will be fine."

Each night I closed my eyes hoping I would not have to use the prescription. I eventually found that access to the medication had the effect Dr. Leo predicted. For me, knowing the bottle was available made me feel safe regardless of whether or not I needed it.

As for the bottle of Ativan, it moved to a new medicine cabinet but held the same pill count as it did when my father picked it up from the pharmacy. Eventually it expired and ended up in the trash. It became an option I never used, transforming from a source of comfort into a symbol of hope.

BEYOND MY GRASP

Love can be a fiction.
—Isabel Allende

I had my first brush with death at the tender age of two.

It happened right after a Mother's Day lunch. After the meal, my family and I walked over to a nearby water fountain. I was fascinated by the water. It looked so beautiful in the sunlight: the water trickling down, seemingly appearing from the spouts out of nowhere. Then I saw something glittering from the bottom of the water fountain. Small, copper circles. I kept inching closer and closer, eager to get my hands on those little round objects strewn across the bottom of the fountain.

The next minute, I stuck my hand into the water, unable to resist the pennies.

"Don't stick your hand in too far," my mother said to me.

I continued to inch forward, ignoring her warnings.

As I stuck my hand farther into the water, I suddenly found the rest of my body submerged. Within seconds, I could barely breathe. I plunged down, deeper into the water. My arms flailed, desperately trying to grab someone or something. My attempts caused water to splash as the sunlight continued shining on my skin.

A moment later, I was pulled from the water by my mother. Her blue silk dress was drenched from the waist down. I caught my breath and let out a cry. I had almost drowned. Those shiny pennies were not as easy to grasp as they appeared and it was then that I learned an important lesson: Looks can be deceiving.

———

This story resurfaced when I was in my early twenties. I had spent the weekend having tough conversations about the future with my girl-friend, Carrie. As we strolled through the park on a beautiful summer night—the temperature was warm with a slight breeze—I longed to reach a satisfying resolution. Fear began to rise as I pondered the future. I worried that I would lose the woman that, at the time, I believed I loved.

We walked through the park and eventually approached the water fountain—the same one where I nearly drowned when I was a child. Despite the fact that more than a decade had elapsed since I last saw this fountain, it was exactly as I had remembered it. Time had preserved this place, and it felt like the fountain was a symbol of my survival.

We sat quietly, gazing into each other's eyes, reenacting a scene found in countless romantic dramas. As I launched into a retelling of my fountain story, I tailored the message to fit our circumstances. Even though I thought I was drowning, I told her, I never gave up. My arms had thrashed, desperate to hold onto something. "I don't quit,"

Samuel Moore-Sobel

I said. "And I am never going to give up on us."

Silence fell over our conversation. Only in the quiet did everything become clear. In that moment, it felt like there was nowhere else we would rather be. I leaned in for our first kiss. It felt like something out of a movie: a moment full of romance and promise for the future. It all seemed too good to be true.

———

The next few months unfolded like a dream. Carrie and I spent hours on the phone sharing our lives and stories with each other. Our level of intimacy grew through each and every conversation. Oh, the joy of being in a relationship. Of uttering every thought, feeling, and occurrence. Of sharing life with someone. Somehow, every breath felt more meaningful, every decision more important. Being with her helped me feel like my life was more significant.

At the onset of our relationship, Carrie asked a lot of questions about the accident, prompting me to explain more about the experience than I typically did with others. In the beginning, I struggled to strike the right balance between revealing too much and conveying the depth of my experience. Oftentimes, her questions caught me off guard, and I shared more than I had originally intended.

I felt inadequate for any woman because of my scars. This didn't change with Carrie. The joy I felt over finding someone who desired me was outweighed by my fears. I was fearful of rejection, of getting hurt, and, ultimately, of losing our relationship. I had determined that my scars, both the visible and invisible effects of the accident, would mean that no one would want to be with me. The more Carrie got to know me, I thought, the more she would want to leave.

Despite the joy I felt in our budding relationship, red flags surfaced from the beginning. Just days after making our relationship public—by changing our relationship status on Facebook, of course—she showed me a text she had received from an old flame. "I hope I didn't get in the way of anything," he had said. She assured him that he didn't, relaying the same sentiment to me as we discussed the events of that day.

Her old flame happened to be a childhood friend of mine, which further complicated the situation. Carrie and I discussed her previous relationship with him ad nauseam. She revealed the details of their affair, making it seem as if their physical encounters had been unwanted on her part.

Despite the fact that Carrie and her ex had their relationship before I came into the picture, I found her account of what had happened deeply troubling. The situation felt unjust, and I was angry on her behalf. We bonded over a mutual hatred of her ex, talking of him often whenever she brought him up. She continually inserted him into our conversations which, over time, started to feel strange. Yet I chose to ignore my misgivings, convincing myself that she was simply trying to heal from past trauma.

As our relationship unfolded, she revealed more and more about her past. The more she told me, the more overwhelmed and unqualified I felt to support her as she shared her deep, unresolved pain. There were moments when I felt I was in over my head until I remembered the sweet words she uttered just two weeks into our relationship.

"I love you," she had said over the phone.

"I love you, too," I said, brimming with excitement over this new development.

After she uttered those three simple words, nothing else mattered. I could hardly believe that she wanted to be with me. She loved me, scars and all. I was determined to love her in the same way.

———

That summer, Carrie came to visit me. My family and I were excited to spend time with her. I thought it might be a way to convince my family and friends of the viability of our relationship. I had heard murmurings of discontent in my social circles—friends and family had expressed displeasure at the way she treated me. I thought this visit might just be enough to win everyone over.

Unfortunately, the trip was a disaster. Her dislike of my family made everyone uncomfortable, and her lack of social graces when it came to meeting family friends ruffled more than a few feathers. As the trip progressed, I did my best to salvage the experience by convincing my family to spend more time with her. A few nights before her scheduled departure, we all decided to watch the movie *What About Bob?*

Carrie and I sat together on the couch that night, my arm around her shoulders. My father, mother, sister, and brother sat nearby. Just moments before the movie began, Carrie unexpectedly received a suggestive text from her ex. I looked down at her phone, unsure of whether or not she wanted me to see the message. After she noticed that I had seen it, our eyes met. She let out a heavy sigh and looked away, grabbing hold of a nearby pillow.

A pit welled up in my stomach as I processed the text message. I couldn't help but wonder whether she was cheating on me. A darkness fell over us as I contemplated next steps. I couldn't say anything to her because my family was right there. We sat in silence while watching the movie. Rather than laughing with my family, I silently counted the minutes until the movie was over.

Once the movie ended, we finally got away and sat on the front porch where we could be alone. Darkness extended across the street as the lights did little to illuminate the road. The hot, muggy air felt sticky as I breathed in and out. I couldn't calm the anger welling up inside me. Carrie repeatedly insisted that this was not what it seemed; the text was simply a reference to an encounter that took place before she and I started dating. I was not so sure, and even if she was telling the truth, considering the lewd text he had just sent her, I did not know why she was still communicating with him. She was angry that I suggested she was cheating on me. As our conversation unfolded, I felt smaller with each passing minute.

Eventually, her repeated denials convinced me that she wasn't cheating on me. Despite that, I asked to be the only man in her life. I reminded her that this had not been the first time an ex had reached out to her during our relationship. The men kept coming back, entering stage left at the most inopportune times. I asked her to refrain from talking to all of her previous romantic partners, highlighting the need for us to start anew. She hesitated. As we sat across from each other on my parents' porch, our argument carried on into the night. I asked her repeatedly to choose me.

Finally, I threatened to end the relationship. I motioned toward the front door, suddenly realizing the humiliation of spending the last few hours begging her to choose me. She relented, finally promising to block all of her exes. I breathed a sigh of relief, grateful that we didn't have to break up.

We parted ways for the night and I climbed into bed, mulling over our heated exchange. Sleep evaded me. I tossed and turned. I stared at the ceiling wondering why she had been so hesitant to choose me. I wanted to feel free from the weight on my chest. I closed my eyes, wondering if I had picked the wrong girl to love.

———

Samuel Moore-Sobel

We broke up. She called me in tears a few days later saying she was devastated by the end of our relationship. One moment she threatened to kill herself if we didn't get back together. The next moment she was blaming me for our breakup, insinuating that I should be the one making amends.

"I want to be with you on that day," Carrie said, referring to the upcoming anniversary of the accident. She promised me a full-scale celebration.

I acquiesced and we got back together. She arrived on September 1 in a dress, driving hours to see me for dinner. We sat down at a familiar restaurant from my childhood, things still a bit awkward after our phone conversation just days before. We attempted to talk things through, agreeing to create a list of qualities we wished the other person would develop.

The exercise reduced the tension between us, and we picked up where we left off before the breakup. We ended the night by doing what we did best—making out in the cool night air, satisfying our physical desires despite the emotional chasm separating us.

Later that night, my parents expressed their displeasure when I finally admitted that I had had dinner with Carrie on September 1. To them, it felt like a rejection. They had been there for every step of my journey toward recovery, yet I had chosen to spend the anniversary of the accident with someone else.

But as my tongue met Carrie's underneath the night sky, I felt no concern about how my family would react. For the first time since our breakup, I felt nearly whole again. After making out, before Carrie reached for her car door to leave, she looked into my eyes and said, "This will always be the day we celebrate getting back together."

I nodded in agreement, touched by the romance of the moment. It wasn't until later that I realized how the intended purpose of that day was not to celebrate a reconnection after a breakup, but to celebrate my life after a near death experience.

We broke up again a few weeks later. We kept talking after the breakup, then stopped. Then talked a bit more, then stopped again. I felt relieved each time we stopped talking. That is until a wave of regret washed over me, mainly over the ways in which my scars had been seen—both visible and invisible—and the ways in which I had shared the most vulnerable parts of myself with her. I regretted sharing those parts of myself with Carrie and the misleading attachment we experienced as a result.

One night, my mother came into my room and sat on the edge of my bed as I recounted a painful experience from my relationship with Carrie. I thought that perhaps, if I kept retelling the stories, I would come to understand what went wrong. Rearranging the sequence of events in my head, I tried to make sense of the relationship.

My mother listened quietly, looking at me as I retold a story she had likely heard before.

As I finished my monologue, I asked her a question that had been on my mind for months.

"Was I in love with her?" I asked, even though I already knew the answer.

"No," she said. She went on to explain that my relationship with Carrie was like a Jeep leaving marks in the dirt as it forged a path ahead. The marks symbolized the ways in which I was wounded by my relationship with Carrie. My brain couldn't let go of the hurt because it was etched into me like the marks from the Jeep.

"Sometimes I think it is hard to get over the track marks," my mother said.

CHOOSING TO SOAR BEYOND

Whatever you are, be a good one.
—Abraham Lincoln

After beginning my college career at Drexel University, I transferred to George Mason University. This course of events made my father prouder than I ever could have imagined. He loved having me live at home, which I chose to do to save money. He also felt strongly that I should attend a college in my home state. George Mason fit the bill.

But I didn't transfer to George Mason to make my dad proud (although that was a pleasant side effect). From a financial perspective, being able to qualify for in-state tuition meant that I wouldn't have to take out additional student loans. Yet another reason I decided to transfer was that I was still attending appointments for my face. I was still seeing Dr. Michaels, a man who seemed untouched by age in the nearly two years I had known him. Despite my declarations of never having another surgery, an operation was planned for Christmas break after my first semester of college. I got sick right before surgery, preventing me from going through with the operation. Regardless, I determined that it didn't make sense to live in Philadelphia when so much of my life was still in Virginia.

Eventually, after three and a half years, I graduated from George Mason University with a degree in Government and International Politics. I was eager to make my way in the world and be free from the high school and college years—especially the surgeries, appointments, and scars that came with those years.

I began my first job with a large consulting company and adjusted to life as a young adult. With each passing year, living with my scars became more bearable. We entered a sort of truce, my scars and I. It wasn't exactly peace or acceptance, but more of a careful easing of hard feelings. In many ways, my life had largely turned out the way it likely would have if the accident had never occurred. I felt a gratefulness for the life I had, even if that meant I still had scars.

But something was still missing. Even with time, I still felt like I needed to find other burn survivors like myself. I wanted to hear their stories and find out if their experiences were anything like mine. Most of all, I wanted to know what it was like for them to live with their scars years after they formed.

I was somewhat familiar with an organization called the Phoenix Society for Burn Survivors. The organization offered scholarships to burn survivors. I had applied for and was awarded a Phoenix Education Grant (PEG) as a senior in high school. I was informed of my selection by the creator of the scholarship fund, Barbara Kammerer Quayle, who called to congratulate me personally. I could hear the excitement in her voice as she relayed this wonderful news. Her kindness shown through the phone as she asked me thoughtful questions and wished me well.

While our conversation was short, the impact she made upon my life was indelible. Being granted this scholarship went far beyond the award itself—it articulated that my story was among an ornate tapestry of many others. Now that I was out of school, I wanted to get in touch with this organization and learn more about it.

That day came nearly eight years after the accident. Years before, as a senior in high school, I had started writing a monthly column for a local newspaper in my hometown. I enjoyed taking on new topics each month, usually pulling material from my own life to share with my readers. Over the years, I've also been able to use my column as a vehicle to highlight important causes.

By far some of the most meaningful words I have ever written were captured when I featured the Phoenix Society in my monthly newspaper column. I interviewed Amy Acton, the organization's executive director. We talked for more than an hour as she shared bits of her own journey as a burn survivor and described the work of the Phoenix Society. The conversation changed my life. I wrote a two-part column from our conversation in which I tried to capture the beauty of Acton's words and sentiments. Acton and I kept in touch by e-mail and she suggested that I attend the Phoenix Society's annual event, the World Burn Congress.

"Will you be able to break away to join us at Phoenix World Burn Congress this year? Look forward to meeting," she wrote in July. The conference was just a few months away, scheduled to take place that fall in Dallas, Texas.

Sure enough, I decided to go. Eight years after sustaining second- and third-degree burns, I attended my first World Burn Congress. My mother accompanied me as we traveled to take part in the largest annual gathering of burn survivors in the world. We flew to Dallas for the five-day conference. I didn't know what to expect from the event. My nerves set in the moment I walked into the hotel. I encountered several groups of burn survivors as I made my way to the front desk.

I started to panic. *What if my scars aren't visible enough?* I wondered. *Would other burn survivors not think of me as a "legitimate" survivor if their burns were more serious than mine?*

I felt tense as my mother and I made our way to our first event: a reception to which Amy Acton had invited us. As we rode the elevator to the event, a woman stood next to us dressed in elegant attire. She spoke with a group of people as we huddled in close quarters. The doors opened and we all walked toward the check-in table. I took my nametag for the event and noticed that the woman from the elevator also took her nametag. It read: Barbara Kammerer Quayle. I recognized the name of the woman who had informed me over the phone several years before that I had been awarded a PEG scholarship. We had only ever spoken over the phone—I was surprised to be standing next to her in person.

My mother and I approached her and introduced ourselves.

"You might not remember me," I said to Barbara, "but we spoke on the phone several years ago when I was awarded a PEG scholarship."

A look of recognition dawned on Barbara's face and she became even more animated than before. She said she was glad to meet me in person. She wanted to know all about my education: what school I had attended, when I had graduated, and where I was working. She seemed pleased to hear about all that had happened since our phone call years before, and she quickly pulled me into a hug. My mother took a picture of us standing together before we were whisked away to the next event.

It is hard to put the experience of attending Phoenix World Burn Congress into words. I heard compelling stories and attended sessions that filled in the gaps of my own emotional journey toward healing. But it wasn't just the empowering words offered by speakers or the care with which others seemed to treat me. It was also the sense that the people at the conference truly, authentically cared about burn survivors. For the first time since the accident, I felt as if I belonged somewhere. I didn't have to explain my face or experience anyone's confused or off-putting comments about my appearance.

Within minutes of meeting Amy Acton, she asked if we were planning to participate in the next activity, which happened to be outside. "I know it's hot," she said, going on to acknowledge the trouble many burn survivors have when exposed to high temperatures. Extended periods of time in the heat can be extremely uncomfortable for me, sometimes even making my scars swell. The rubbery feeling on my face is exacerbated by heat, and my face often begins to itch. With Amy and others at the conference, I didn't have to explain any of this. How liberating it felt to walk into a room full of people whose life experience mirrored my own.

I found that some of my struggles were also shared by other young adults at the conference. Many of us were wondering whether anyone would love us in spite of our scars. We struggled with feeling misunderstood and had been forced to grapple with rude and insensitive remarks from others along our journeys. I even heard others echo what I had tried to tell Dr. Leo years before—that other young people, too, wanted a romantic partner who knew them before their injuries. I tried to soak up every moment of the conference. I didn't want to forget a single thing.

The following words were printed on a large banner prominently displayed in the hotel lobby: #burnsarebeautiful. I marveled at the sea of people who willingly took pictures of themselves in front of the sign. I was still trying to avoid cameras even years after the accident. Many of my most important memories went unrecorded as I continued to duck away from the camera. But this day was different. I stood in front of the banner and flashed a smile while my mother took a picture.

She couldn't help but smile, too. "You've never looked so at peace," she said.

WELCOME BACK TO GOING UNDER THE KNIFE

Let her cover the mark as she will, the pang
of it will always be in her heart.
—Nathaniel Hawthorne, *The Scarlet Letter*

Before I attended the World Burn Congress, I had noticed that my right nostril seemed to be getting pulled down, constricting my airway as a result. I noticed it during long runs when my lungs would heave as I attempted to get more oxygen. But the hardest moments were at night. Years of facial surgeries had conditioned me to sleep on my back. I would lie face up with two pillows under my head, and it felt like I was suffocating right before falling asleep. That would make me breathe even harder, struggling to have adequate air flow into my right nostril. My parents suggested that I see a plastic surgeon, but I had vowed to never have another surgery. I had kept this promise now for more than six years.

Attending World Burn Congress softened my view on the matter.

At the conference, I met a medical professional who recommended a few plastic surgeons with experience working with burn survivors. I was heartened to learn that there were a few in the Washington, D.C. area and was surprised that we had not learned of them before. I was intrigued by the possibility of treatment from a doctor who was familiar with burns. Buoyed by the conference, my openness to exploring surgery grew.

I made an appointment with a doctor in McLean, Virginia. Much to my surprise, the wait was shorter than I expected. The nurse led me to a room, and in walked the surgeon, Dr. Barry Cohen.

"Hello," Dr. Cohen said as he greeted my mother and me. He wore a white button-down shirt, but the buttons were undone almost halfway down his chest. His unorthodox appearance made me feel a little nervous. I braced myself for disappointment.

I told my story, and Dr. Cohen was attentive, asking thoughtful questions about my injuries along the way. I shared my medical history, detailing my previous surgeries. He listened intently, refraining from interrupting or interjecting.

After I answered all of his questions, he asked to examine my face. He did not seem alarmed by what he observed. In fact, he seemed surprised that the damage was not worse.

"It looks like you got in a bike accident or something—not that you suffered second- and third-degree burns," he said.

His work with burn survivors, he said, was motivated by his experience during his medical residency. He had spent years molding the faces of burn survivors who had traumatic marks. He shared interactions he'd had with other patients, and those whose injuries were far worse than my own.

He told a moving story of another burn survivor whose accident was caused by a malicious street encounter. As the patient walked through the city, a stranger threw sulfuric acid in his face. The survivor became blind. His wife was pregnant at the time, and the accident meant he could never see his child.

The story brought tears to my eyes. I felt deep gratitude that I had not lost my eyesight as a result of the accident. I shuddered to think about how it would feel to never see the people I loved.

At one point, he discussed memory loss as a result of burn injuries.

"Many experience amnesia," he said, noting that burn survivors sometimes cannot remember key details about their injuries or trauma.

He asked, "Do you remember anything?"

"Yes," I said, able to recall almost every detail.

As our conversation progressed, I felt more and more comfortable with Dr. Cohen. I wanted to ask a question that had been on my mind ever since September 1, 2009. I couldn't stop thinking about how the surgical team at the hospital, on the day of my accident, didn't seem to know what they were doing. Hence why they had to call the hospital next door just to carry out my debridement surgery.

"Would my recovery have been better if I had been taken to a different hospital?" I asked him.

I wanted to know if my face would look different if I had not had the skin graft, which was subsequently removed. Or if I had been treated by plastic surgeons who specialized in burns. What I really wanted to know was if my face would look different if I had encountered Dr. Cohen years before.

"The outcome wouldn't have been any different," Dr. Cohen responded. "You are really lucky in the outcome." Upon hearing his answer, I felt relieved.

Then Dr. Cohen broached the possibility of surgery. He outlined a plan of action, articulating his desire to focus on the scar under my nose, while trying to excise my chin. Lastly, he said he would apply a laser to all of my remaining scars to dull the redness.

As he described his plans, I felt an unexpected burst of excitement. Dr. Cohen seemed up to the task, and I felt like he could improve my quality of life. Once he addressed my fears about what could go wrong, I was ready to sign up for another operation. Although some questions remained. "Would I need more surgeries?" I asked.

"I can get you eighty to ninety percent there," Dr. Cohen told me with the caveat that a few minor operations might still be required. He also mentioned that the sides of my face would likely not age at the same rate.

He predicted that as I grew older, "The right side of your face will look like you got a facelift."

This sounded unpleasant, but I decided to cross that bridge when I got to it.

We talked for a bit longer, his gentle responses easing my concerns about another surgery. He spent more than thirty minutes with my mother and me answering all of our questions. As the questions began to slow down, he offered a few heartfelt words before we parted.

"I am here to serve you. I do this for the soul," he said.

———

On the day of the surgery, a nurse led me into the operating center. By now, I had the pre-surgery routine down pat. I changed into a dressing gown and sat on the hospital bed. The nurses placed an IV in my arm without too much resistance from my rolling veins. At some point, Dr. Cohen arrived for a visit to review his plans for the operation with me and my mother.

"What I'm going to try to do is take a little tissue from here," he said, pointing to my cheek. "I want to open up the nostril for you," he continued, "because you are missing tissue from that right side."

He indicated where he would provide laser treatment and predicted the length of the surgery.

"It's not going to take a long time," he said. "I think it will be better," a reference to my previous experiences with surgical procedures.

He indicated his plan to laser "residual burns" along with the nasal labial fold. We pointed out a few other areas, asking if he was willing to treat those as well. "Whatever you want," he said.

"Anything else? Did I miss anything?" he asked.

He had identified each scar, eleven in all. I had no more scars to show him.

"So vestibuloplasty to your nose, fix your chin, laser the rest," he said.

He looked down, rifling through the papers on the desk.

"Minimal to no pain, that's good news, right?" he said, almost as an afterthought.

And with that, he was off. Soon after, the anesthesiologist arrived. She explained how I would be put to sleep, and I began to ask a series of questions.

I had conducted research about anesthesiology before. I was worried about the possible side effects, and its sometimes fatal consequences. One of the most frightening possibilities I discovered was vomiting during surgery, which could cause fluid to shoot into my lungs and interrupt breathing.

I shared my concerns with the doctor.

"You haven't eaten anything," the anesthesiologist said, communicating that vomiting during surgery only applied in scenarios when patients eat shortly beforehand.

"Well, I feel better," I said. But I still had questions.

"As far as hydration," I asked, "should I drink a lot after the surgery?"

I often knew the answer to my questions before I asked, but asking the questions allowed me to process my emotions and nerves. I wanted the doctor to reassure me that everything would be okay.

I asked how long the surgery would be, eager to see if her answer would match the one given by Dr. Cohen just minutes before.

"An hour, hour and a half?" I asked.

"Yeah, I don't even think it's going to be that long," she said. By now, she had probably begun to think that the surgery would be far shorter than the time it was taking to answer all of my questions.

She promised I would wake up quickly once I reached the recovery room, reiterating that she expected the surgery to be short. Then, as if urging me along the journey, she said the words I was anxiously trying to avoid: "We are all set to go if you are ready."

I asked if I could use the restroom. In addition to relieving myself, I wanted to have one last look at my face before surgery. I knew that the next time I looked at my face, it would be different.

"Get a hug," the anesthesiologist said, motioning towards my mother, who was sitting nearby.

"Ok," I said.

Turning to my mother, I said, "Love you."

"Always and forever," she said.

"If I don't make it, just know I love you," I said.

"You're gonna . . . you're gonna be fine," my mother said.

A nurse who had been in and out of the room all morning overheard our exchange. She had been privy to my pre-surgery routine, which included my last-minute declarations of love to my family members just in case I didn't make it through the operation.

"Oh, Lord," the nurse said. "You will be fine."

A nurse wheeled me toward the bathroom and helped me get inside. Once I got into the bathroom, I looked in the mirror, eager to get one last look at my face. This was the face that had been crafted by different doctors over several years, carefully carved, etched, shaped, and mended. I took one look at the scars under my nose, chin, and neck. I felt the need to say goodbye. I was parting ways with the face I had come to know. This face, with all of its imperfections, was one to which I had become accustomed. The one that had greeted me each morning when I looked into the mirror for the last several years. Although I longed for a different face, somehow, I would miss this one.

When I emerged from the bathroom, a nurse led me back to the room. I crawled into bed, and the nurse draped a blanket over me. I still felt worried, but I tried my best to be brave. At this point, it was time for courage.

The nurse asked once again what part of my body was to be operated on and asked a few questions.

"How did this happen to you?" she asked me.

Even right before surgery, I couldn't escape this question. As the anesthesiologist began the IV drip, I shared my story—a brief version that likely became more muddled with each passing second.

I thought preparing for surgery would get easier each time. In my case, years of practice did little to lessen my pre-surgical anxiety.

As I prepared for surgery, I remembered what someone had once told me: "You are no longer in the throes of this terrible accident." I realized again the truth of this statement. My life was different from what it once was. I had climbed mountains, weathered storms, and come out on the other side. Even if I would never have the face I wanted, I was grateful for my life. I had been gifted with an excellent doctor to work on my face. I had been graciously born into a family that loved me unconditionally. And ultimately, I could rejoice in the reality of being alive when I once faced death. I pondered these things as my consciousness faded and the medical staff guided me toward the promise of a new beginning.

"Where is the doctor?" I asked as my consciousness continued to fade.

The nurses told me he would be in shortly. I resolved to stay awake until he arrived. I kept talking, desperate to preserve my consciousness. I could hear myself stumbling over my words as my eyesight began to fade, and the world around me blurred. The nurse warned me that I was about to fall sleep. I felt a sense of peace. I reminded myself that choosing to undergo one last surgery was the right decision. I would keep fighting to restore what was lost, just as I was fighting in that moment to keep my eyes open. Despite my best efforts, the battle was soon lost as my eyes closed without my permission.

THE MISSING PUZZLE PIECE

Et tu, Brute?
—William Shakespeare, "Julius Caesar"

Even several years after the accident, time had failed to clear up certain mysteries. For instance, who did the sulfuric acid belong to and why had it been in the shed that day? Years before, the woman who owned the property where the accident took place claimed that the sulfuric acid belonged to her ex-husband, yet the identity of her ex-husband had never been revealed. In my mind, he was a mystery, and I assumed he always would be.

As I was conducting research to write this book, I visited my old high school in the suburbs of Virginia. It was nearly three years after I graduated from high school. I was back, but this time on my own terms. I felt a sense of déjà vu as I walked through the double doors. It felt strange to roam the halls again.

I bristled as I walked past the auditorium, remembering what it felt like to be a teenager. I recalled trying to piece together a life that hardly made sense, coming to grips with parts of myself and my experience that I didn't like.

My mother accompanied me as I made my way to the back of the school that day. We had conducted interviews with numerous teachers and faculty who had been involved in my return to school after the accident. I had come to see Mr. Dade, a member of the school administration. I was eager to fill in some of the gaps of my memory and to learn more about the role he and the school staff played during my high school years.

Soon after we arrived, Mr. Dade appeared. He made his way over to us, displaying a toothy grin. A tall, soft-spoken man, his voice had a distinctive hoarse quality. He was engaging and charismatic, and his sunny demeanor made me feel good whenever I talked to him.

He escorted us to his office and directed us to sit in the chairs across from his desk. Since it was spring break, school was not in session. I noticed that Mr. Dade's hair had receded in the years since I had seen him last, and his eyes looked more tired than I remembered.

My mother and I took turns asking questions, starting out by asking him for general memories of my time at the high school.

"The way he carried himself made it hard not to love the kid," Mr. Dade said with a hint of emotion.

He went on, sharing his response upon finding out about the accident for the first time. "We were going to do everything we could to help him," he said.

As the interview progressed, it became clear that he knew more about me than I had anticipated. He recalled my sense of self, commitment to my faith, and tight-knit family—he saw those as reasons I was able to overcome the aftermath of the accident.

He also said that a network of teachers and students had been willing to jump in and help me during those days. Unfortunately, during that time I had felt mostly unsupported by the network he was referencing.

He said that most people in the school had been asking, "What can we do to make things better for this kid?"

He also shared what other teachers thought about me. "Mrs. Allen thought you were the best thing ever," he said.

His high praise began to make me uncomfortable and my hopes of learning more about what happened behind the scenes within the school administration after the accident began to wane. Until suddenly, Mr. Dade paused.

"There are several pieces to it," he said, referencing my case.

He then dropped a name of a teacher who worked at the school. He said that this particular teacher had come to visit Mr. Dade a few days after the accident. I gathered, from what Mr. Dade said, that this teacher had told him about an accident that had injured a minor on his ex-wife's property.

"He was such a mess—and he said, 'The student is in this building,'" Mr. Dade recounted.

Initially, I was confused as to why Mr. Dade was referencing this teacher who I had never taken a class with in high school. *What was Mr. Dade insinuating?* I wondered.

"The teacher never mentioned your name," Mr. Dade continued. He then went on to describe this teacher.

Mr. Dade, in a rather confusing way, was referencing an interaction that he had just days after the accident with the ex-husband of the woman in possession of the sulfuric acid that burned my face and arms. The jar the woman had claimed belonged to this teacher. As I listened to Mr. Dade, all I could think about was the fact that, throughout my high school career, I had unknowingly come into contact with the man who was, at the very least, partially responsible for my injuries.

It remained unclear to me how close of a friendship Mr. Dade had maintained with this teacher. I wasn't even sure why Mr. Dade was telling us this information. It seemed like Mr. Dade thought that my family and I had known that this teacher was the woman's ex-husband from the beginning. Of course, we had not.

I was incredulous. I told Mr. Dade that I couldn't believe this information had been kept from us. Why had we not been notified from the beginning that this teacher—the man who had stored the sulfuric acid so carelessly, the man arguably most responsible for my injuries—worked at my high school?

Mr. Dade hedged before steering our conversation back to his interaction with this teacher just days after the accident.

"The teacher was so visibly distraught—he sat in the very chairs you sit in now. I had never seen him sit in a chair and cry," Mr. Dade explained.

I was silent. I didn't know what to say. My mother jumped in, telling Mr. Dade that we would have made very different decisions if this information had been shared years before. For one, I never would have returned to this high school.

Mr. Dade looked shocked.

I began to think through my memories. I remembered this teacher—the owner of the sulfuric acid—in several situations from my high school years. I remembered passing him in the lunchroom. I remembered seeing him in the hallway. I remembered that he had a tendency to appear in my classrooms at odd moments. In hindsight, it seemed like this teacher had been tracking my story and progress from the periphery—as if he was, without my knowledge or permission, watching me recover throughout my high school years.

Whether I knew it at the time or not, the very man who had set me and my family on this painful course had been watching all along. How could our lives be so inextricably linked, yet fully without my knowledge?

I wondered if he had lurked at the outer edges of my high school years in order to free himself from guilt. He would have watched me talk to friends in the cafeteria, get passing grades in my classes, and graduate on time. I wondered if this soothed his sense of responsibility and guilt. It felt like he got what he wanted: closure and freedom from any pangs of conscience, knowing that I had gone on to survive. But I never received what I wanted: a clear and honest explanation for why the acid was stored in that shed in the first place.

Suddenly, another memory came to mind. I remembered this teacher's repeated presence in my study hall classroom during my sophomore year—the study hall that Mr. Drake had rearranged my schedule so I could attend. Was it possible that I had been switched into that study hall just so that this man could watch me?

I asked Mr. Dade this question.

"I didn't know about that," he said, appearing uncomfortable.

I felt betrayed and angry. I could not believe that Mr. Dade was defending this teacher. Just minutes before, Mr. Dade had claimed to be one of my greatest supporters in high school, but now it felt like he was defending the man who inadvertently hurt me. I struggled to reconcile Mr. Dade's words with his actions. My last question remained: Did this teacher's tears matter more than my own? Did his tears matter more than my scars? "People need to be seen for who they are," he said, in a comment directed to my mother. "That's not who Sam is," he continued, referencing my burns. "And that's not what he did for our school."

I never did find out why this teacher stored the sulfuric acid the way he did. Perhaps Mr. Dade did not know, or perhaps he did. The teacher in question was not teaching chemistry to high school students, nor was he affiliated with any other science-related subjects (as far as we knew). Just as his identity had remained a mystery for years, so were the reasons behind the placement of that glass jar.

ONE LAST APPOINTMENT

Every new beginning comes from some other beginning's end.
—Seneca

In several post-surgery follow-up appointments with Dr. Cohen, he appeared to be pleased by my progress. The improvement in my breathing was worth celebrating, and I felt optimistic by how much better this round of surgery had gone.

Still, there was some room for improvement with my face. Dr. Cohen mentioned the possibility of carrying out another operation, one that "would take about twenty to thirty minutes." It could be done in his office without anesthesia. The operation would create additional airflow by extracting cartilage from my ear and placing it under my nose.

However, in my last appointment with Dr. Cohen, he offered another possibility.

"I know my burn patients get tired of getting cut open," he said.

"Yes, I've had a bunch of those over the years," I said.

"I know," he said.

I struggled over what to do next. The possibility of increased airflow was appealing, but the idea of another operation was not. I wanted to end this chapter of my life, leave surgery behind and move on to whatever came next.

"It's up to you," Dr. Cohen said.

He said that as I continued getting used to my new face, I could decide over the next few months whether or not additional surgery would improve my quality of life. Regardless, Dr. Cohen would still be willing to treat me.

"If you want to improve your breathing you can call us and we can schedule it," he said.

As our appointment came to a close, he offered one last bit of advice.

"Live your life," he said.

And just like that, I was free. Free from more surgeries, from reflecting upon what-ifs, and from reliving the accident. For the first time in nearly nine years, I was free, in some ways, from the accident itself.

I walked out of Dr. Cohen's office and was greeted by the cool, mid-morning air. I crossed the street and walked toward my car, finally free to begin anew.

Only one question remained: What now?

FINALLY MEETING A FRIENDLY FACE

OK, enough already . . . let's go back to where we were.
—Bob Timberg, *Blue Eyed Boy: A Memoir*

"Hi, I'm Bob," the man said. He had a kind face with soft eyes. The man was Bob Timberg, a successful journalist and author known for books such as *The Nightingale's Song* and *John McCain: An American Odyssey*. He built a career as a writer for *The Baltimore Sun*, earning accolades for his work, such as his coverage of the Iran-Contra affair. However, my interest in him extended beyond his journalistic work. I wanted to know more about the tragedy that nearly ended his life.

Days before, I had heard his voice on my car radio during an interview on NPR. He spoke quickly, as if he didn't have a lot of time. He had a smooth voice that was soothing to the ear and spoke about his new book, *Blue-Eyed Boy: A Memoir*. After years of prodding, he had finally sat down to pen the story about his tragedy.

He set the scene—one that took place nearly forty years before.

Thirteen days before Bob was scheduled to return home from serving in Vietnam, he was sent into town to retrieve paychecks for his unit. The twenty-six-year-old Marine could not wait to return home to see his wife, Janie. Then the vehicle he was traveling on hit a land-mine, and Timberg was engulfed in flames. The hot, red fire severely damaged his face and body. He incurred deep physical and emotional scars as a result. When he returned home, he endured more than thirty surgeries throughout a long and painful recovery.

"I looked like a monster," he told radio listeners on that summer afternoon.

I determined then and there as I drove along the highway to find a way to meet this man. Fortuitously, Washington, D.C. had a book-store that was one of the first stops along Bob's book tour. I decided to attend the event.

When it was time for the event, I was eager to catch a glimpse of Bob—someone who knew what it meant to experience tragedy and survive. I approached his table that evening, hoping that he would spend a few moments with me.

When our gaze met, I could not help but notice the intense blue of his eyes. I kept looking at them, unable to draw myself away from their depth and pain. I wanted to see him for who he was and avoid focusing on his scars. I took great pains not to react at the sight of his scars and was committed to maintaining eye contact for our conver-sation. My story spilled out when I shook hands with Bob.

"I was in an accident involving sulfuric acid," I told him.

He let out a gasp in response. As I continued sharing my story, he leaned in, looking incredulously at my scars. Recognition flashed across his face the moment his eyes reached the scar under my nose. He continued to search my face, looking up and down in order to detect any remnant of trauma.

"Sulfuric acid, huh?" he said, as if trying to understand my story.

"Well, the other guy got it worse, right?" He smiled.

His heartfelt words created a moment of understanding between us.

I told him that although we had important differences between our stories, I could relate to much of what he had shared. I identified with his feelings of anger and loneliness in the aftermath of trauma, his determination to survive in the face of adversity, and his willingness to keep going, even if the future remained uncertain.

He nodded his head. He seemed to understand my story and was able to grapple with the pain of my past. I marveled at his ability to communicate empathy with his eyes. Trauma has a way of binding people together. After many years of meeting people who were baffled by my experience, Bob's brief look of understanding was like an oasis in a desert.

"You look good," he told me over and over.

I grabbed a book from the table for him to sign.

"Who should I make this out to?" he asked.

"Samuel," I said shakily, nearly overcome by the emotion of the moment.

His head shot up with a look of amazement.

"Samuel is the name of my son."

We shook hands. I caught one last glimpse of his blue eyes. Turning away from Bob, I made my way toward the register. Carefully opening the cover of the book, I scanned the first page for a quick glimpse.

"To Samuel—who knows about comebacks."

EPILOGUE
SEPTEMBER 1, 2019: A NOTE ON THE TEN-YEAR ANNIVERSARY OF THE ACCIDENT

It is never too late to be what you might have been.

—George Eliot

It is hard to put into words how I feel ten years after the day my life changed forever.

In many ways, the accident is no longer a part of my daily experience. I have gone on to buy a home, build a career, and reach many of the milestones that mark adulthood. I have even found someone to love, someone who loves me back: a beautiful, wonderful girl who I intend to marry.

Yet despite how different my life looks today in comparison to ten years ago, plenty of reminders of the past still exist. To this day, my scars are often the first attribute people notice about me. I still receive questions from strangers and acquaintances about my appearance, and I am still, even to those who have known me for nearly a lifetime, often remembered as the boy whose face was burned. No matter how the rest of my life unfolds, I may always be that boy.

While I have gone on to experience many adventures since my teenage years, the accident is still the most notable, life-altering, and traumatic experience of my life. This event has shaped my worldview and forced me to re-evaluate many areas of my life. I had to come to grips with not only how I looked and how I felt, but also how to decipher the meaning of the scars I carry.

I have learned through this experience that scars not only identify past struggle, but present triumph. I no longer live in fear of what others will say to me, nor do I continually dwell on what I lost. I do my best to wake up each morning and praise God for the gift of life that He has given me. No matter what happens over the course of a day, I can rest in the knowledge that joy is within reach, even in the midst of adversity.

During my high school years, I used to ask God to take away my scars. Nearly every morning during the moment of silence in my high school, I bowed my head and ran my hand over the red marks, praying for my face to be restored.

I no longer ask God to take away my scars. As the years have unfolded, a journey without scars becomes harder to imagine. Wishing for them to disappear feels like wishing away a part of myself. Nowadays, I'm not sure I'd be willing to part with my scars. They are a part of me now, a part of my story that I no longer want to eradicate.

Despite the growth and healing I've experienced, I still live with the consequences of the accident. I still have to be careful about spending too much time in the sun. When I do venture out, I have to apply copious amount of sunscreen and wear a hat. I use a Neti Pot to drain my sinuses each morning and many nights while regularly taking a slew of vitamins to combat my propensity for sinus infections.

Much of what lies ahead, as it pertains to my injuries, remains unknown. How my sinuses will react in the future after such high exposure to sulfuric acid remains a mystery. Early on, doctors said my risk for skin cancer was high. Dr. Cohen's prediction of an unintended "facelift" on half of my face remains unappealing. As has been true along so much of this journey, a lack of answers is par for the course.

Yet, despite this, I am determined to carry on. I want to share this story to maybe help others, while doing my best to live a life worthy of the one I have been given.

I would be remiss if I did not admit that a part of me still longs for the full restoration of my face. I will likely always feel that way. Yet my sense of longing lessens with each passing year. After years of wrestling, I feel as if I have finally come to peace with myself. Perhaps when Jim Maxim shared with me that it took ten years to heal, he was speaking of something far deeper than his physical appearance.

Writing this book has been one of the most challenging, gut-wrenching, and all-encompassing experiences of my life. I have poured my heart and soul into this work, and have spent years trying to determine what to say and how to say it.

I remember a conversation I had a few years ago after sharing my story with a group. A woman from the audience approached me, and said, "I was diagnosed with something chronic. I needed to hear what you said tonight. You gave me hope."

Such words have stuck with me in the intervening years. They remind me of the power of hope, the importance of sharing our stories with others, and how we need each other in our journeys toward healing. I humbly submit my story to you, and I hope you'll do the same by sharing your story with others. I believe that the world can be changed, one story at a time.

It starts with you.

ACKNOWLEDGEMENTS

I never could have done this without my mother, father, brother, and sister.

They were there for me every step of the way: from the moment my injuries were sustained to the present day. I have felt their love throughout this long journey. I have cherished the ways in which they have encouraged me, heard me, and seen me. Without them, none of this would have ever been possible.

My mother is a remarkable woman. She has spent her life sacrificing for others, especially when it comes to her children. Her intentional mothering, spiritual insight, intellectual curiosity, encouraging words, and unconditional love helped me to become the man I am today. Her editing and collaboration on this project helped to bring this story to life. She encouraged me to keep writing even when I was tempted to give up. I could never have asked for a better mother.

I am grateful to my beautiful fiancée, Megan, who so graciously edited this manuscript four times. I will be forever appreciative of her efforts and will cherish the joy and happiness that she has brought into my life from the very first day that we met. She is the most beautiful, intriguing, and kind woman I have ever encountered. I admire her strength of character and commitment to those she loves. Her gentle presence has effectively put to rest all of my fears, worries, and anxieties about finding someone to love. How could I have ever known that I was waiting for her all along?

A special thank you to Mascot Books for taking a chance on an unpublished author with little more than a story to tell.

To Mrs. Allen, who always believed in me.

To Dr. Barry Cohen, an excellent surgeon who never failed to treat me with kindness and respect.

To the Phoenix Society, specifically Amy Acton. She is a remarkable woman who shares so much of herself with everyone she encounters. The work being done by this vital organization is near and dear to my heart, and I'm determined to spend the rest of my life supporting this worthy cause.

A special shout-out to my editor, Valerie Cury, who started publishing my column in the *Blue Ridge Leader* when I was just a senior in high school and has been graciously doing so ever since. Her support and words of encouragement have meant the world to me.

A heartfelt thanks to Danielle Nadler, who wrote the very first newspaper article about the accident when I was just a senior in high school. Her efforts helped me to believe that others would want to read my story.

To Zayde—who always understood. To my friend Griffin, who gave me permission to include him in my book. To Dr. Leo, who taught me the importance of using reason when grappling with powerful emotions.

I could go on and on, but I'll end by saying how grateful I am to the countless others who encouraged me along this journey. The supportive friends, mentors, teachers, and professors who all did their best to offer words of encouragement and support. Thank you.

ABOUT THE AUTHOR

Samuel Moore-Sobel is a writer, speaker, and community activist. His work has been published in *Burn Support Magazine*, *Open: Journal of Arts & Letters*, *Loudoun Times-Mirror*, *Loudoun Now*, and other publications. He is a columnist for the *Blue Ridge Leader* and previously served on the local disability services board. He writes about trauma, his experience as a burn survivor, faith, and political activism. When not writing and speaking, he works in the tech industry. He graduated from George Mason University with a degree in government and international politics. He currently lives in Loudoun County, Virginia. Read more at his website: samuelmoore-sobel.com.